UNKNOWN
MASTERPIECES OF
INDIAN FOLK & TRIBAL ART

FROM THE PERSONAL COLLECTION OF K.C. ARYAN

UNKNOWN MASTERPIECES OF INDIAN FOLK & TRIBAL ART

Subhashini Aryan

K.C. ARYAN'S
HOME OF FOLK ART
Museum of Folk, Tribal & Neglected Art

First published in India in 2005 by B.N. Aryan,
Director, K.C. Aryan's Home of Folk Art,
Gurgaon.

Text and photographs © 2005 by
K.C. Aryan's Home of Folk Art
Museum of Folk, Tribal and Neglected Art
2009, Sector 4, Urban Estate
Gurgaon-122 001, Haryana, INDIA

Tele/Fax: 91-124-2321783

www.museumoffolkandtribalart.org

ISBN: 81-901933-0-9

Design
Kirti Trivedi

Photography
Anup Sood & Fotographics, Delhi

Printed and bound by
Ajanta Offset Ltd., New Delhi

K. C. ARYAN
(1919–2002)

A great visionary whose single-minded and lifetime
devotion and personal labour bestowed on Indian folk
and tribal art the glory it deserved. His perceptive mind
and encyclopaedic vision ensured for Indian folk and
tribal art a place at par with courtly arts.

This work is dedicated as a tribute to his great passion
and concern for India's folk and tribal artistic heritage.

**SPENT NEVER A MOMENT IN PURSUIT OF REWARD
MIND AND HEART NEVER SOUGHT AN AWARD
LIFE WAS BUT A DEDICATION TO ART
AND DEATH ITS FINALE**

न छानी ख़ाक दर-दर की
किसी ईनाम के ख़ातिर
जिये भी काम के ख़ातिर
मरे भी काम के ख़ातिर

ACKNOWLEDGEMENTS

Our most profound gratitude and sincere thanks go to the Swedish International Developement Co-operation Agency (Sida), Stockholm, Sweden, Embassy of Sweden, New Delhi and the Department of Culture (Ministry of Tourism and Culture), Government of India, New Delhi who left no stone unturned in turning this dream into reality, by extending their kind funding support towards publishing this magnum opus.

Special thanks are due to Mr. Sudhir Jain and Mr. G.D. Aryan for their unfailing support, co-operation and wisdom at every stage.

Contents

Life size head of a tribal woman cast in dhokra technique, Bastar, late 19th century. H. 29 cm.

INTRODUCTION

HOME OF FOLK ART is at present housed in its former Founder-Chairman, late K.C.Aryan's personal residence at Gurgaon, a suburban town adjacent to South Delhi, and within easy distance from the Indira Gandhi International Airport in New Delhi. Established in 1984 by K.C.Aryan, an internationally renowned modern painter, sculptor, art historian and art collector, it contains one of the world's finest collections of Indian folk and tribal arts. The quality and scope of this extraordinary collection give us an insight into the out-of-ordinary creative and aesthetic vision and dauntless determination of the great modern artist. The timelessness of these art forms, the universal language they speak, and the unbroken continuity of their dynamic and versatile tradition stirred his imagination. He brought to bear his personal creativity and connoisseurship to shape his vast collection. His predilection for the most unusual, rare and unexplored, the unknown and little known enabled him to reach out to these artifacts, about the existence of which even the art world was unaware.

K.C.Aryan was a great visionary. As early as the 30s and 40s, when he was instinctively drawn to the artifacts of rural and tribal flavour, he was greatly disturbed by the non chalance, attitude of gross neglect, condescension and despise on the part of the museum authorities and connoisseurs of art. What prompted him to build such a wealth of collection? Innumerable priceless bronze icons of Hindu deities that once were venerated most fervently by the natives on their home altars were being melted down to be shaped anew into utensils or were discarded and thrown away into the rivers, lakes, oceans or local ponds. Countless precious manuscripts got eaten up by the termites and perished for good. Other artifacts met the same tragic fate. Aryan was deeply hurt by this callous vandalism. He realised that if no effort was made to save this unique treasure, it would be lost forever. He tried speaking to his influential friends in the art circles of Delhi, scholars and connoisseurs of art, but his appeals fell on deaf ears. In spite of lack of adequate financial resources and space at his disposal, he pooled together all his money and energy over a span of seven decades to build this enormous collection.

In the course of time, his collection grew so large that he had no choice but to display a part of it in his own personal residence, and named it HOME OF FOLK ART : MUSEUM OF FOLK, TRIBAL AND NEGLECTED ART. "But why neglected art? Once these artifacts are preserved, they are no longer neglected," contended most visitors. The vast and varied collection of K.C.Aryan consists of numerous art and craft forms that have never attracted any collector's eye. Hence the tag 'neglected'. Secondly, numerous artifacts are no longer being created; their traditions have become extinct, and they can be seen only in K.C.Aryan's personal museum.

K.C.Aryan's aim was not merely to preserve these artifacts for posterity, to prevent them from getting irretrievably lost, but also to accord them the status they most richly deserve. The museums all over India house art objects in courtly styles, bearing dynastic names such as Maurya, Sunga, Gupta, Gurjara-Pratihara, Chalukya, Chola, Pallava, etc. Greater preference is accorded to paintings and sculptures created by artists attached to the royal courts over the centuries. Artifacts from rural and tribal India were outrightly dismissed as everyday objects, completely unfit for display in a museum. No one, with the sole exception of K.C. Aryan, realised that the illiterate and unknown craftsmen living and working in the countryside had nurtured our artistic and cultural heritage since hoary antiquity, and preserved it from getting lost for good. If at all, certain objects of everyday use were collected by a museum, they were relegated to the category of 'decorative arts', anthropological and ethnographical material. K.C.Aryan reacted strongly to these prevailing trends, and eventually succeeded in achieving his target.

The collection was built painstakingly, with exceptional perseverence and patience, in spite of K.C.Aryan's modest means. He was no business tycoon, never had much money. But the idea of preserving this priceless and timeless artistic heritage kept goading him on and on…. In fact, it was built at great personal and family sacrifice. He gave away his all to salvage for posterity whatever he could afford to buy.

The uniqueness of this museum lies in its priceless collection of rare and unusual objets d'art from all over India. However, special focus is on the Punjab, Himachal Pradesh and Haryana, the three provinces often dismissed and shrugged off as being completely devoid of any artistic and cultural expression worth the name. K.C.Aryan not only collected artifacts from these places, but also wrote books on them.* Numerous art objects that have already become extinct can be seen in this collection.

*A complete list of K.C. Aryan and S. Aryan's books is being given at the end with a view to enable the readers to know the wide range of themes attempted by them.

In the course of time, Aryan transcended the geographical limits he had imposed upon himself. He collected art objects and artifacts purely for their aesthetic merit, irrespective of their provenance. This way, his collection did not remain confined only to Punjab, Himachal and Haryana, but became a national treasure, containing representative examples of rural and tribal artifacts from all over the sub-continent.

K.C.Aryan's predilection for amazingly bold, spontaneously shaped, dynamic creations of the rural and tribal folk that project their creators' direct vision, unstamped by external influences was innate. His profound fascination for them since his early childhood days grew stronger and stronger, as he advanced in age. In the course of his travels, off-the-beaten-tracks, he handpicked artifacts that appealed to his artist's discerning and trained eyes.

K.C.Aryan ranks amongst the foremost pioneers who raised their lone voice for the cause of folk and tribal artifacts, and will always be remembered for his path-breaking efforts and invaluable contributions to this noble cause. As early as 1973, he placed the folk bronzes of our country on the world's artistic and cultural map by his trail-blazing magnum opus FOLK BRONZES OF NORTH WESTERN INDIA .

The second revised edition of this book was published in 1991 as INDIAN FOLK BRONZES, and opened the eyes of the world art historians, scholars and connoisseurs of art to the beauties and subtle stylistic nuances of Indian folk bronzes. Until then, no one, not even Indian scholars, was aware of their existence. Only thereafter, the craze for collecting these long-eclipsed art objects began, both at home and abroad.

It is sad to note that over the centuries, much of the wealth of artifacts of folk and tribal variety has been irretrievably lost for obvious reasons : indiscriminate vandalism, wilful destruction, neglect, and lack of awareness of their value and significance on the part of their owners. Till now, it is unfortunate that this heritage is still being dismissed to the category of utilitarian objects. By and large, Indians have not realised that they bear the impress of our collective consciousness.

Besides preservation and dissemination of knowledge regarding folk and tribal artifacts, K.C.Aryan had set out greater goals for himself: he wanted to educate the masses so as to enable them to understand their significance as cultural links, to instil in them the idea not to destroy them or allow them to perish. He wished to mobilise public opinion, awaken a sense of pride in them, and to undertake pilot conservation projects. According to Aryan, "had it not been for these artisans living and working in the rural and tribal pockets, our precious artistic and cultural heritage would not have survived. The dynastic or courtly arts relied upon royal patronage, and lasted as long as the political fortunes of the rulers favoured them. Gaps in our knowledge of the history of courtly arts exist. While the political fortunes of the rajas ebbed and flowed, the rural and tribal art forms continued to be shaped by the artisans in an unbroken continuity, flowing on and on unhindered like a stream. The peaceful living conditions in the rural and tribal pockets remained unaffected by the political upheavals and invasions. Besides, the rural-tribal craftsmen enjoyed complete socio-economic security."

The factor that contributes immensely to the significance of this museum collection is the transformation the rural and tribal art forms are undergoing in the present age of globalisation, industrialisation and urbanisation. The Madhubani painting being produced and sold these days is nowhere near its original counterpart, that is preserved in our museum. The same is true of tribal art forms . Since countless artifacts have already perished or fallen into disuse, the museum collection will serve as an important point of reference, an invaluable source of information and knowledge about an interesting aspect of our rural and tribal artistic and cultural heritage, and eventually will become an important resource centre of education and culture.

The scope of K.C.Aryan`s collection is exceptional, with over 2500 years of rural and tribal artifacts represented. It is essential to clarify here that these art objects have no history, and the oldest object extant does not go beyond the early 18th century. The sole exception, however, are the bronze icons of Hindu deities, going back to the tenth century A.D. The terracotta figurines, curiously, bear the unmistakable stamp of timelessness. A figurine of the Mother Goddess in this medium in our collection is datable to the fourth century B.C.. By displaying this historically significant example, K.C.Aryan desired to drive home to the visitors the message of their unbroken continuity till the present day. Curiously, the terracotta objects shaped over the centuries continued to be fashioned in the rural style, and their remarkable affinities with the folk bronzes impress one and all, and enable them to visualise the art forms created by artisans in the twin mediums in the remote antiquity.

The museum is equipped with a well stocked reference library, with a vast collection of art books and journals. It also has a large photographic archives containing over 1,50,000 photographs, black and white, colour prints and transparencies for the benefit of scholars and researchers. So far, a part of the museum collection has been exhibited twice : in 1986 at the AIFACS galleries in New Delhi, and in 1991, at the Government Museum Annexe,

Chandigarh, under the auspices of North Zone Cultural Centre, Patiala. The museum is visited by researchers from all over India and abroad. Renowned art historians have used art objects from our museum collection for their books such as :

Heinz Mode : Indian Folk Art, Mumbai; 1980.

Pupul Jayakar : The Earthern Drum, New Delhi; 1978.

Vidya Dehejia : The Chaunsath Yoginis, New Delhi; 1986.

Barbara Rossi : From the Ocean of Painting, OUP, New York; 1998

And many more.......

List of books by K.C. Aryan & S. Aryan

Indian Folk Bronzes – K.C. Aryan

Hanuman: Art, Mythology & Folklore – K.C. & S.Aryan

The Aryans: History of Vedic Period – K.C. & S. Aryan

SKY: Sadhana Kala Yatra, an autobiography by K.C. Aryan

Encyclopedia of Indian Art: References, symbols and
   Evolution of Devanagari Script – K.C. Aryan

Rural Art of the Western Himalaya – K.C. & S. Aryan

Basis of Decorative Element in Indian Art – K.C. Aryan

The Little Goddesses – Matrikas – K.C. Aryan

The Cultural Heritage of Punjab, 3000 BC – 1947 AD – K.C. Aryan

Punjab Murals – K.C. Aryan

100 Years Survey of Punjab Painting, 1841-1941 – K.C. Aryan

Crafts of Himachal Pradesh – S. Aryan

Himadri Temples, A.D. 700 – 1300 – S. Aryan

Folk Embroidery of Himachal Pradesh – S.Aryan

Folk Bronzes of Rajasthan – S. Aryan

Unknown Pahari Wall Paintings from North India – K.C.Aryan

Indian Decorative Designs – Kamla Aryan

RURAL AND TRIBAL ARTS:
THEIR SIGNIFICANCE

India is a land of villages, from where originated all our art forms. Paintings, sculptures, architecture, music, dance, drama, and a host of hand-crafted objects – all sprang from the indigenous soil. From the earliest times, our distinctive culture has played a significant role in the unification of our country and her people. In spite of the multiplicity or plurality of dialects, languages, seasons, the turns of phrases or proverbs, which form the poetry of rural parlance, are identical all over the country. The village well or tank is the hub of the local community's social life.

All through the length and breadth of our vast subcontinent – it would not be impertinent here to assert that even areas that no longer form part of our country, but originally did – the ritualistic and utilitarian artifacts that have been created in the past, and are still being shaped, in every medium, display designs, motifs, symbols, thematic content that share a baffling commonality, even if the objets d`art appear to have a distinctive identity and style all their own. The traditionalist craftsmen draw upon the same repertoire for ornamental patterns and designs, as well as for themes, since art is inseparable from religion. The artist dedicated his talent and skill to God. He meditated long before creating a sculpture or painting, and transferred his spiritual-aesthetic vision to visual or plastic language. In this respect, the rural craftsmen were by no means different from their counterparts working under the royal patronage. It has often been stressed by many a writer that rural arts are the creations of untutored hands. Those who write like this only display their ignorance of the facts. The craftsmen living and working in the countryside are illiterate in the modern sense of the term, but they are not completely unlettered in the traditional sense. They were fully conversant with their religious lore, i.e. the puranic literature, the Ramayana, the Mahabharata, the legends revolving around Shiva, Durga, Vishnu and their manifestations, with the tenets of the shilpa shastras, with iconography and iconology, like their more accomplished, sophisticated courtly brethren. Like the latter too, the rural artisans inherited their craft traditions, skills, technical knowledge and expertise, and training from their fathers or grandfathers, and transmitted the same to their descendents in turn, and in this manner, our centuries-old traditional artistic and cultural heritage has remained alive till the present times. Over the centuries, these artifacts of rural and tribal flavour have served as visual documents, essential means of human communication, conveying a deep sense of our age-old tradition and inspired potential of their creators.

The rural art forms are an indelirable link between the artistic output of the countryside and the courtly, aristocratic arts that found expression at Ajanta, Ellora, Elephanta, and innumerable structural temples, royal palaces and noblemen's mansions. However, as the cultural and artistic backbone of the community that nurtured it, it was the only tangible link between various communities – rural as well as tribal – in days when writing for the masses was yet unknown. These art forms, apart from their utilitarian value, also served to educate the illiterate masses in their country's religious literary texts as well as folk and tribal lore. All over India, the artists evolved audio-visual techniques for this purpose. For example, in Maharashtra, the chitrakathis (artist-narrators) painted album sets of the Ramayana, the Mahabharata and puranic legends of Shiva, Durga and Vishnu in and around Paithan (ancient Pratishthanpur), which they showed to the rural audiences in the evenings by travelling from village to village. The masks, string puppets from Rajasthan , leather puppets from Andhra Pradesh and South India, the pata chitras from Orissa, the phad paintings from Rajasthan, the pichhwais from Nathdwara in Rajasthan, Kalighat paintings, the scroll paintings executed by the jadu-patuas of Bengal, the large painted fabric hangings popularly known as Mata-no-chandarvo from Gujarat, and a large number of similar objects combined entertainment with education. The same function was performed by innumerable terracotta and bronze figurines, steeped as they were in religious, folk and tribal lore. The housewives shaped the clay images of the Hindu deities for worship on diverse occasions, when they observed fasts for their family and children's well being, prosperity and longevity. The rural and tribal warriors were deified and venerated , their bronze or terracotta equestrian figurines were placed at the family altars, or at a place specially chosen by the village community elders under a tree or in the local shrine compound.

Apart from the religious texts, non-religious texts were also illustrated by the rural artists. These pictorial expressions are marked by vibrant colours, bold brush strokes, unbelievable spontaneity, dynamism, and minimal use of colours, preferences being for primary colours, primal forms, and imaginative use of space. The figures – divine, human or any other – might be somewhat archaic, disproportionate, crude, nonetheless, not devoid of an indescribable charm; their bold imaginativeness has a haunting quality that can be experienced, but not expressed in verbal language.

The mudwalls of rural homes share most of the pictorial elements described above. The thresholds are daily decorated anew with impressive ornamental, but profoundly symbolic patterns all over India, known variously as chowk-poorana in Punjab and Haryana, likhnu in Himachal Pradesh, rangoli in Uttar Pradesh, alpana in Bengal, mandana in Rajasthan, etc. The urge to adorn one's body in a variety of ways such as painting, tattoo designs, silver ornaments, attractively embroidered garments for each and every member of the family as well as for embellishing the walls of their homes with hangings, ceilings with canopies, the main entrances of residential houses with impressively designed toranas – appliqued, embroidered or made of beads – contributed to the richness and colourfulness of the family and social ambience. Ritual ceremonies, cycles of seasons, fairs and festivals lent an additional colour and richness to their otherwise drab lives. The day-to-day swinging community life enjoyed by the ruralfolk as well as their tribal kinsmen go a long way to render their lives meaningful, by filling them with laughter, gaiety, cheerfulness – all these factors have a definite bearing on all their creations, be it painting, image-making, singing or dancing.

The winds of change sweeping through the country due to exposure to urbanisation, modern education that is completely unrelated to their own socio-cultural milieu, industrialisation and now the latest rage of globalisation have rapidly brought about transformations in the life-styles of rural and tribal folk. In their case, "ignorance is bliss" is more apt an expression. Their artistic and cultural moorings have become shaky. In this respect, our vast collection, combined with diverse activities of our museum, will render a yeoman's service to our great nation by instilling in our compatriots a sense of pride and awareness of this somewhat neglected, but precious, artistic heritage.

Dr. Subhashini Aryan
CHAIRPERSON

Bronzes

● 1
Eight-armed Durga
Mahishasuramardini
(bronze icon), Shimla hills,
Himachal Pradesh;
late 16th century.
H. 29.5 cm.

2
Four-armed Durga
Mahishasuramardini
(bronze icon), Shimla
hills, Himachal Pradesh;
13th-14th century.
H. 21.5 cm.

3
Four-armed Durga
Mahishasuramardini,
Shimla Hills, Himachal
Pradesh; 17th century.
H. 17 cm.

● **4**
Durga riding on her lion
vahana, Himachal Pradesh;
17th century. H. 12 cm.

● **5**
A very powerful bronze
icon of eight-armed Durga
astride the lion. Chamba,
Himachal Pradesh;
17th century. H. 14 cm.

● 7
Eight-armed Durga in
a standing posture,
Himachal Pradesh;
17th century. H. 6 cm.

● 6
Four-armed Durga
Mahishasuramardini,
Shimla hills, Himachal
Pradesh; 14th century.
H. 17 cm.

8
Eight-armed Durga
Mahishasuramardini,
Kulu, Himachal Pradesh;
16th century. H. 16.5 cm.

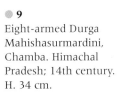

9
Eight-armed Durga
Mahishasurmardini,
Chamba. Himachal
Pradesh; 14th century.
H. 34 cm.

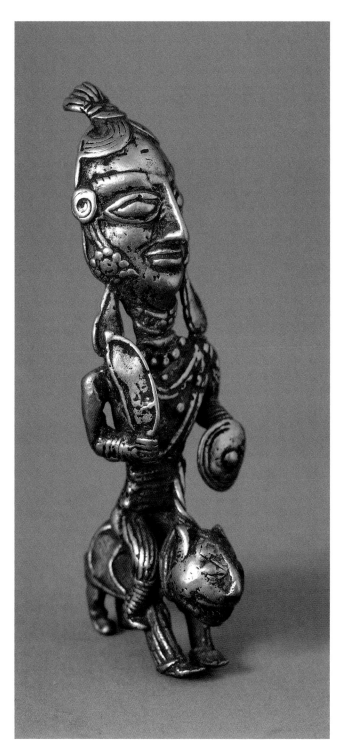

10
Durga Simhavahini, wielding a sword and a shield, Himachal Pradesh, 15th century. H. 13 cm.

11 *right*
Four-armed Durga Mahishasuramardini, Shimla hills, Himachal Pradesh. 17th century. H. 14 cm.

12
Four-armed Durga Mahishasuramardini, Shimla hills, Himachal Pradesh; 14th century. H. 22.5 cm.

● **13**
Four-armed Durga
Mahishasuramardini,
Shimla hills, Himachal
Pradesh; 15th century.
H. 18.5 cm.

● **14**
Six-armed Durga
Mahishasuramardini,
Shimla hills, Himachal
Pradesh; 14th century.
A very grotesque
bronze icon. H. 11.5 cm.

15
Four-armed Durga
Mahishasuramardini,
Shimla hills,
Himachal Pradesh;
16th century.
H. 16 cm.

16
Four-armed Durga
Mahishasuramardini,
Himachal Pradesh;
15th century. H. 16.5 cm.

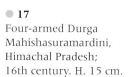

17
Four-armed Durga
Mahishasuramardini,
Himachal Pradesh;
16th century. H. 15 cm.

18
Four-armed Durga
Mahishasuramardini,
Shimla hills, Himachal
Pradesh; 15th century.
H. 14.5 cm.

19
Four-armed Durga
Mahishasuramardini,
Orissa; 15th century.
The panchratha
pedestal has affinities
with bronze icons cast
in courtly tradition.
H. 14.5 cm.

21
Ten-armed Durga
Mahishasuramardini,
Orissa, 16th century.
H. 13 cm.

20
A very unusual
depiction of Durga
Mahishasuramardini,
Himachal Pradesh;
16th century.
H. 7.5 cm.

22
Eight-armed
Durga Mahishasuramardini,
Maharashtra; 18th century.
H. 21 cm.

23
Eight-armed Durga
Mahishasuramardini,
Maharashtra;
18th century. H. 12 cm.

24
Eight-armed Durga
Mahishasuramardini,
Maharashtra; 18th century.
H. 12.5 cm.

25
Eight-armed Durga
Mahishasuramardini,
Maharashtra; 18th century.
The goddess's eyes are studded
with rubies. H. 16 cm.

26
A lustrous, dynamic bronze
icon of eight-armed Durga
Mahishasuramardini,
Maharashtra; 18th century.
H. 17 cm.

27
Archaic yet moving bronze icon
of Durga Mahishasuramardini,
Himachal Pradesh;
16th century. H. 11.5 cm.

28
Bronze icon of a
Mother Goddess
sitting in an
unusual posture;
provenance
unknown, 18th
century. H. 12 cm.

30
Four-armed Goddess Durga
standing, her right foot placed
on the back of her lion vahana
in front, Maharashtra;
17th century. H. 12 cm.

29
Ferocious,
blood-thirsty
Goddess Kali,
Madhya Pradesh;
19th century.
H. 17.5 cm.

31

A rare portrayal of Narasimha emanating from a pillar split into two parts to kill demon Hiranyakashipu, lying prostrate on the god's knees. Chamba, Himachal Pradesh; 10th century. H. 11.5 cm.

32

An unusual chiselled icon of Durga Simhavahini, Rajasthan; 18th century. H. 11.5 cm.

33
Four-armed Shiva holding a staff, a bowl, etc. in standing posture; in addition to a garland, the folds of his full-length dhoti have been delineated carefully. Maharashtra; 18th century. H. 7.5 cm.

34
Shiva and Parvati astride Nandi, flanked by a pair of devotees. Himachal Pradesh; 16th century. H. 18.5 cm.

35
Vishnu and Lakshmi astride Garuda, Himachal Pradesh. 16th century. H. 14.5 cm.

36
A highly impressive and
powerful bronze icon of
Gugga Chauhan, deified Rajput
warrior, worshipped as a folk
hero; originally the bronze icon
was painted, traces of which
are still visible, Jodhpur,
Rajasthan; 16th century.
H. 22.5 cm.

37
Equestrian bronze figurine
of a local deified warrior,
Maharashtra; 18th century.
H. 13 cm.

38

A rare bronze icon depicting
boy Krishna followed by his
herd of cows and elder brother
Balaram, Rajasthan;
19th century. 23 x 7 cm.

39

Equestrian figurine of a deified
warrior, Madhya Pradesh;
19th century. H. 16.5 cm.

40

Equestrian figurine of a
deified warrior, Bastar,
Chhattisgarh;
19th century. H. 6 cm.

41

Equestrian figurine of a
deified warrior, Maharashtra;
19th century. H. 9.5 cm.

42
Flautist Krishna standing with crossed legs (bronze). Rajasthan; late 18th century. H. 21.5 cm.

43
Conventional portrayal of flautist Krishna, completely engrossed in the musical rhythm, Maharashtra; 17th century. H. 13 cm.

44
Hanuman challenging
the enemy and
trampling over a demon,
a bronze circular plaque;
shading the god are the
hoods of Shesha;
Maharashtra;
17th century. H. 21 cm.

45
Village deities
(gramadevatas).
Maharashtra;
18th century.
H. 14 cm.

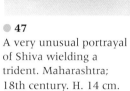

46
Four-armed Shiva with
a staff and bowl,
Maharashtra;
18th century. H. 12 cm.

47
A very unusual portrayal
of Shiva wielding a
trident. Maharashtra;
18th century. H. 14 cm.

48
Bronze icon of a village deity (gram-devata), Maharashtra, 19th century. H. 12 cm.

49
A deified village hero, Rajasthan; 10th century. H. 8.5 cm.

50–51
Deified village heroes (gram-devatas) seated on a high pedestal, Maharashtra, 18th century. H. 8 cm each.

a

● **52–54**
Shiva Lingam flanked by Nandi
the sacred bull and Naga
(serpent). (a & b) 19th century;
11 x 7 cm each, (c) 18th
century; 18 x 12 cm.

b

● **55**
Shiva Lingam flanked by
Nandi and a devotee,
Maharashtra; 19th century.
H. 8 cm.

c

56
Bronze icon of Mother
Goddess – it seems to
have been modelled on
clay figurines of the same
deity, Bengal;
19th century. H. 8 cm.

57
Seated Nandi, Shiva's
sacred bull, on a pedestal,
canopied by Sheshnag.
Maharashtra. 18th century.
H. 39.5 cm.

58
Ekadashmukhi (eleven headed)
Shiva, an extremely rare icon
made of lead, Nasik,
Maharashtra; 19th century.
H. 8 cm.

59
Panchmukhi (five-headed)
Shiva, Maharashtra,
19th century. H. 7.5 cm.

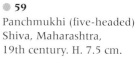

60–61
Panchmukhi (five-headed)
Shiva, astride his Nandi vahana
(images made of lead), Nasik,
Maharashtra; 19th century.
H. 8 cm.

● **62–63**
Equestrian figurines of deified
tribal heroes, Chhattisgarh,
19th century. H. 12 cm & 17 cm.

● **64**
A tribal goddess seated
in crossed-legs posture,
Chhattisgarh,
19th century. H. 30 cm.

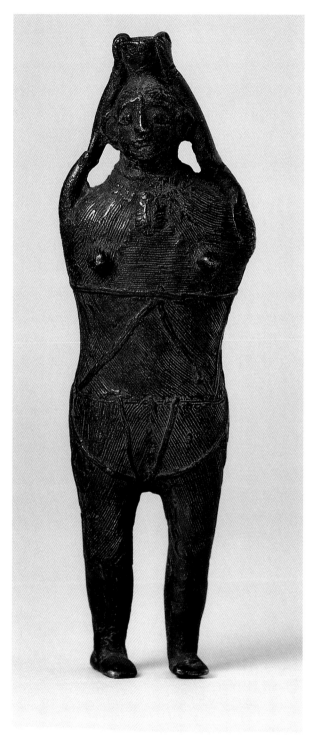

66–68

(66) a deified tribal warrior astride an elephant; H. 15 cm; (67) an equestrian figurine, H. 16 cm., and (68) a pair of tribal heroes riding on horseback, Kutia Kond tribe, Orissa-Andhra border area; early 20th century. H. 8.5 cm.

66

67

68

65

Bronze icon of a tribal woman carrying a basket on her head, Chhattisgarh, 19th century. H. 20 cm.

● **69**
Deified clan ancestors
(bronze), Kutia Kond
tribe, Orissa-Andhra
border area; early 20th
century. H. 15 cm.

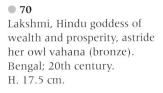

● **71**
A Kutia Kond tribal woman
balancing a pitcher on her
head, Orissa-Andhra border
area; early 20th century.
H. 22 cm.

● **70**
Lakshmi, Hindu goddess of
wealth and prosperity, astride
her owl vahana (bronze).
Bengal; 20th century.
H. 17.5 cm.

● **72–76**
Bronze figurines portraying
horse and elephant riders,
Kutia-Kond tribe, Orissa-
Andhra border area; 20th
century. H. 8 cm; H. 10 cm;
H. 10 cm; H. 8 cm; and H. 8 cm.

77
Goddess Mauli Devi venerated
with much fanfare by the
tribals of Bastar, Chhattisgarh;
19th century. H. 58 cm.

78
Lakshmi, Hindu goddess of prosperity, astride an elephant, Bastar, Chhattisgarh; late 19th century. H. 23.5 cm.

79
Equestrian figurine, Bastar, Chhattisgarh, early 20th century. H. 15 cm.

80

A deified tribal warrior or clan ancestor portrayed along with his spouse holding a baby, all seated on a high pedestal; a pair of animal heads projecting on both the sides, Chhattisgarh; late 19th century. H. 36 cm.

81

A grinning mask-like head sacred to Maria tribe, Bastar, Chhattisgarh, early 20th century. H. 16 cm.

82

Elephant riders, Kutia Kond tribe; 20th century. H. 9 cm.

● **83–84**
Ferocious, bloodthirsty goddess
Kali with a lolling tongue
standing on prostrate Shiva,
(83) Orissa; H. 20 cm;
(84) Bengal; H. 19 cm.
Contemporary.

85
Elongate form of a mother
carrying a baby. Chhattisgarh,
contemporary. H. 22.5 cm.

86
Maria mukuta,
Bastar, Chhattisgarh;
contemporary. H. 87 cm.

● **87**
A tribal bride and bridegroom,
their joined hands indicative of
their marriage rites being
solemnised, Bastar,
Chhattisgarh; late 19th century.
H. 9 cm.

89
Manasa Devi, the serpent-headed tantrik goddess popular in Bengal; 20th century. H. 8.5 cm.

88
A tribal bronze showing a gramdevata with two sticks. Chhattisgarh, late 19th century. H. 10.5 cm.

THE MOHRAS
The Devi (Durga) Masks
(Brass plaques)

Himachal Pradesh

The tradition of casting this kind of plaque-like mohras of Durga and Shiva is prevalent all over Himachal Pradesh and in Uttaranchal, where they are venerated both in the temples and household altars. Their basic function was to serve as processional deities. Such mohras are placed in sedan-chair-like rathas (chariots), decorated with silk garments and floral garlands and taken out in processions on religious festivals like Dussehra, Shivaratri, and annual fairs of the deities.

90
Devi mask
Shimla hills;
13th –14th century.
H. 31 cm.

91
Devi mask
Kulu; 16th century; H. 13 cm.

92
Devi mask
Shimla hills; 16th century;
H. 19.5 cm.

93
Devi mask
Chamba; 16th century;
H. 20.5 cm.

94
Devi mask
Chamba; 15th century;
H. 27 cm.

95
Devi mask
Chamba; late 18th century;
H. 23.5 cm.

96
Devi mask
Kulu; 16th century;
H. 17.5 cm.

97
Devi mask
Shimla hills; 15th century.
H. 23 cm.

● **98**
Stylised Shiva head,
North Karnataka;
18th century. H. 34 cm.

● **99**
Bhairava head,
North Karnataka;
18th century.
H. 29 cm.

|

100
Large stylised Shiva head made
of copper sheet.
North Karnataka; 19th century.
H. 54 cm.

101
Bhairava head,
North Karnataka;
19th century; H. 20 cm.

102
Bhairava head,
North Karnataka;
18th century; H. 30 cm.

103
Bhairava head,
North Karnataka;
19th century; H. 24 cm.

104
Bhairava head,
North Karnataka;
19th century;
H. 28 cm.

● **105**
Mukhalinga, (phallus cover),
Karnataka; 19th century.
H. 23.5 cm.

● **107**
Shiva head, Karnataka;
19th century, made of brass
sheet. H. 43 cm.

● **106**
Bhairava head, Karnataka;
18th century, H. 27 cm.

108–109

The Daksha masks; their remarkable affinities with the traditional dance-dramas such as the Yakshagana deserve to be emphasised. Karnataka; 18th century. H. 17 cm and 18 cm.

● **111**
A Bhuta (Muga) mask
(brass), South Karnataka;
19th century. H. 36 cm.

112
A Bhuta (Muga) mask
(brass), South Karnataka;
19th century. H. 33 cm.

113
Shiva mask, Maharashtra;
19th century. H. 22 cm.

● **114**
Four-armed Ganesh seated
on a high lotus pedestal,
Maharashtra; 17th century.
H. 14 cm.

● **115**
A very archaic bronze icon of
seated Ganesh offset by a
surround and a siras-chakra,
Himachal Pradesh;
17th century. H. 9 cm.

116

An unusual bronze icon of
Ganesh with three trunks and
canopied by a five-hooded
cobra, seated on an elliptical
pedestal, his rat vehicle is
standing with folded hands.
Maharashtra; 19th century.
H. 13 cm.

117

Ganesh seated on a high
pedestal and surrounded by a
beaded ogival aureole,
canopied by a cobra,
Maharashtra; 17th century.
H. 13 cm.

118-119
The elephant-headed
Ganesh seated on a circular
pedestal. Bastar,
Chhattisgarh; late 19th
century. H. 9 cm and 11 cm.

120
Ganesh sitting in an unusual
posture, Himachal Pradesh;
17th century. H. 3 cm.

● 121
Four-armed Ganesh astride
his rat vehicle, Maharashtra;
18th century. H. 16 cm.

123
The Shiva family – Shiva astride his Nandi mount, his spouse Parvati carrying baby Karttikeya and Ganesh – a very unusual theme for a bronze icon, probably inspired by local paintings, Himachal Pradesh.
14th century. H. 10.5 cm.

122
Shiva in standing posture, Himachal Pradesh;
17th century. H. 5.5 cm.

124
The village deities (grama devatas). Maharashtra;
19th century.
H. 12 cm.

126
Human-bodied Garuda with
folded hands in anjali mudra,
Himachal Pradesh;
18th century. H. 25 cm.

125
Garuda in conventional posture, supporting a flat lotus rosette
intended for black stone (saligrama), Vishnu's emblem, Gujarat;
18th century. H. 21 cm.

127
Mother cow feeding calf;
cylindrical form arrests the eye,
Rajasthan,
20th century. H. 3.5 cm.

128
Lingam-Yoni enthroned on a
high pedestal, canopied by an
inordinately large cobra hood,
Maharashtra; late 18th century.
H. 26 cm.

Terracottas,
Papier Mache Crafts

● **129–130**
Painted clay figurines of
famous Rajasthani lovers
Dhola-Maru. Jodhpur,
Rajasthan. Late 19th century.
H. 25 cm and H. 40 cm.

● **131**
Terracotta head of goddess Kali,
Bengal; contemporary.
H. 38 cm.

● **132**
Painted clay head of Issarji
(Shiva) worshipped at the
Gangaur festival, Rajasthan;
19th century. H. 20 cm.

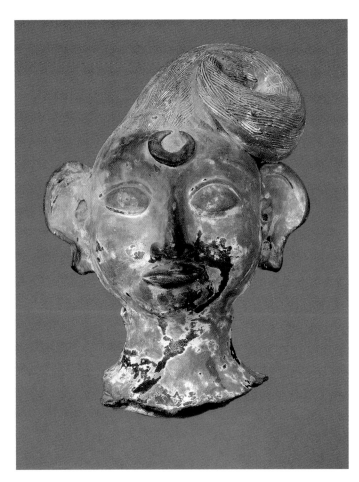

● **134**
A clay toy cart. Haryana;
contemporary. H. 13 cm.

● **133**
Shiva Head (painted terracotta);
Jodhpur; 19th century.
H. 20cm.

● **135**
An elephant rider
(painted clay figurine).
Jodhpur, Rajasthan;
19th century. H. 18 cm

● **136**
Painted clay figurine of Ganesh
Benaras; contemporary.
H. 22 cm.

● **137**
Painted clay figurine of a
female drummer.
Kurukshetra; contemporary.
H. 15 cm.

● **138**
Painted papier-
mache toy.
Bihar,
contemporary.
L. 27.5 cm.

● **139**
A terracotta figurine
of the Mother
Goddess, Bihar,
fourth century B.C.
H. 11 cm

● **140**
Durga Mahishasuramardini
flanked by Lakshmi, Saraswati,
Ganesh and Karttikeya painted on
a clay plaque (shara), Bengal;
contemporary.

● **141**
Painted glazed pottery, Sind;
19th century.

● **142**
Painted clay pottery. Amritsar,
Punjab. Contemporary.
Completely unknown pottery
which used to be sold at the
Ramtirth fair some years ago.

TERRACOTTAS, PAPIER MACHE CRAFTS

77

● **143–144**
Masks of Hanuman
and Durga's lion
vehicle (papier-
mache) Nurpur, H.P.;
20th century.
H. 37 and 39 cm.

● **145–146**
The Ravana mask: iron mould
for making the Ravana effigies
for the Dussehra festival, and
the side mask. Amritsar.
20th century. H. 33 cm &
63 cm.

● **148**
Durga riding on her lion mount carved on a black stone stele, Kangra, H.P. 19th century. H. 19 cm.

● **147**
Ancestor images or memorial stones of clan ancestors for worship. Himachal Pradesh; 19th century. H. 15 cm & 23 cm.

● **149**
Yoni for tantrik worship,
composed of two coconut
shells that grow in this form in
Seychelles Island;
contemporary.

● **150**
A flat seat (Moora) made of
coloured grasses. Chiniot,
Punjab. Designs that appear to
have been inspired by the
phulkaris have been deftly
woven by a housewife.

Puppets &
Ganjifa
Playing Cards

● **151**
Painted card puppets,
Jaisalmer, Rajasthan;
17th century. This specimen
is available only in our
museum collection.

152
Leather puppet of Hanuman
carrying Rama. Andhra
Pradesh; 19th century.

● **153–155**
Painted traditional playing
cards of India (ganjifa sets),
generally circular in shape; the
rectangular ones date from the
Mughal period. Such playing
cards were used all over India,
and kept in a specially designed
wooden box.

154

155

● **156**
Ganjifa set with a specially
designed and painted wooden
box. Maharashtra,
19th century.

Paintings:
Patakas, Tantrik & Folk

PATAKA PAINTINGS

Specimens of Tantrik priests' art seen only in our museum.

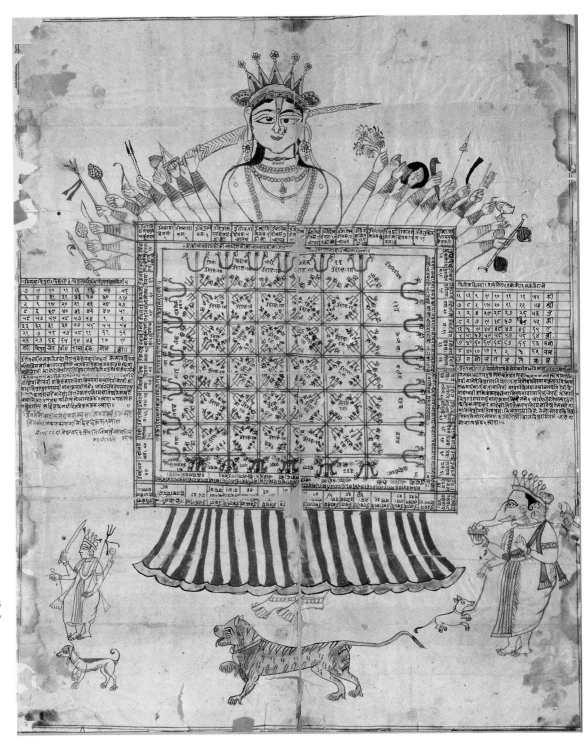

● **157**
Devi pataka, Jodhpur, Rajasthan. Mid-18th century. Inscribed all over with yantras and mantras, these works were painted entirely by the tantrik priests (sadhakas) for personal worship and for attaining spiritual powers (siddhis), without the intervention of professional artists.

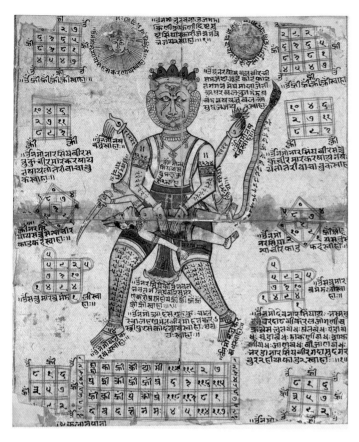

● **158**
Narasimha pataka showing the
Man-lion incarnation of Vishnu
in the act of killing the demon
Hiranyakashipu, Jodhpur,
Rajasthan; mid-18th century.

● **159**
The Jain pataka,
Rajasthan;
18th century.

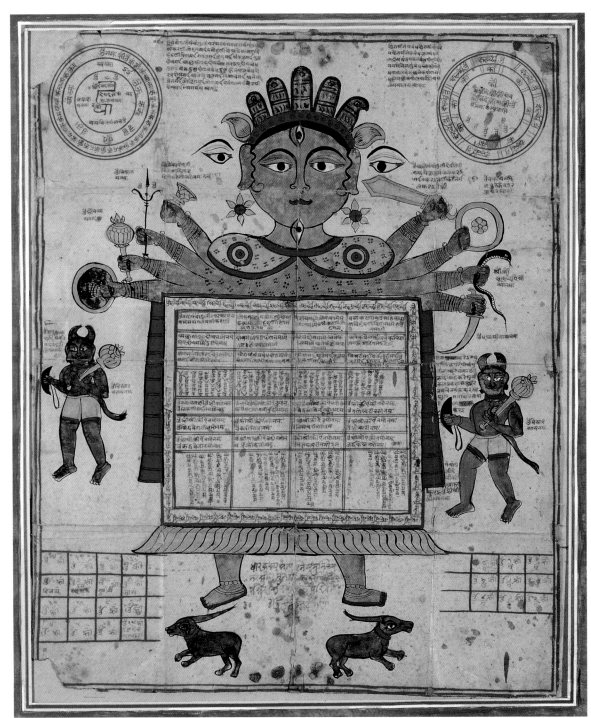

● **160**
Devi pataka,
Jodhpur, Rajasthan;
18th century.
The square form of
the goddess' body is
symbolic of the
Mother Earth.

● **161** *opposite*
Panchmukhi (five-
headed) Hanuman
with multiple arms
and weapons.
Jodhpur, Rajasthan;
18th century. The
female figures being
trampled upon by
the god are
demonesses
vanquished by him,
and also emphasise
the complete self-
control Hanuman
had over his senses.

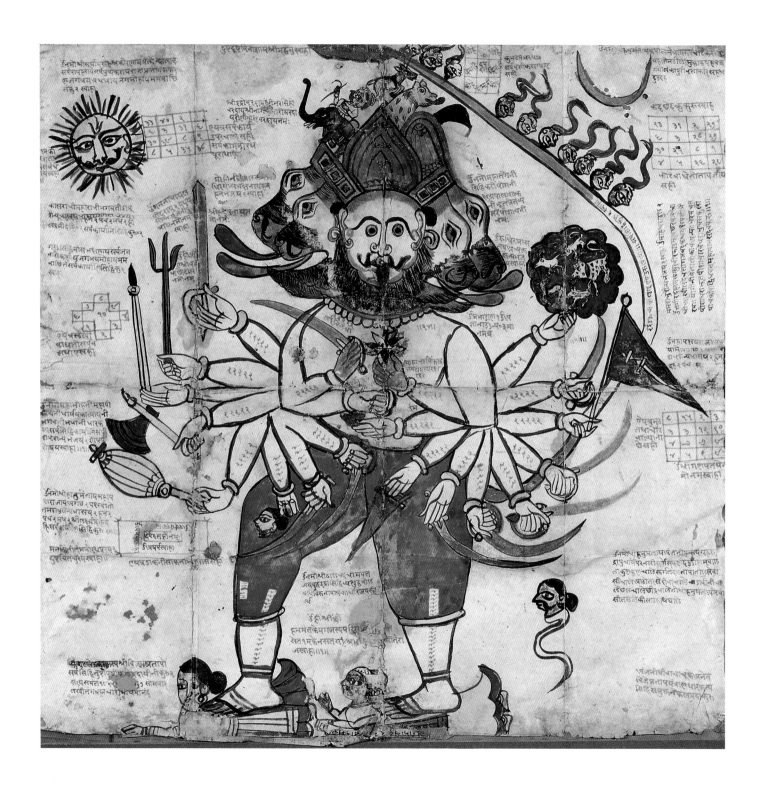

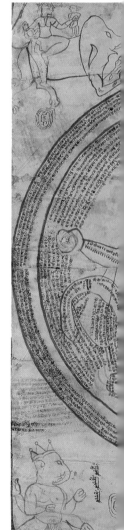

● **162**
A rare portrayal of Hanuman in bold black outline, Uttar Pradesh or Gujarat; 17th century. The inscriptions in Arabic and Gujarati languages indicate that its painter was a muslim tantrik worshipper of Hanuman. This instance of a muslim devotee of a Hindu deity is by no means exceptional.

● **163**
Archaic portrayal of Hanuman enclosed within a mandala, Rajasthan, 18th century.

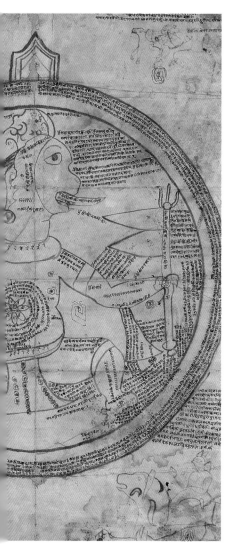

● **164**
The conventional portrayal of
Hanuman, Rajasthan;
18th century. His entire body
is inscribed with mantras,
pertaining to his Lord Shri Ram.

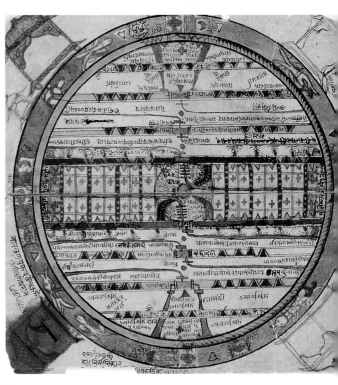

● **165**
Ganapati pataka
inscribed all over with
mantras, Rajasthan,
18th century.

● **166**
The Jambu-dvipa or
India as visualised by
the Jains. Rajasthan.
18th century.

● **167** *opposite*
Devi pataka, Rajasthan; 18th
century. The square body of the
goddess encloses sixty-four
diagrams (yantras) pertaining
to the sixty-four tantrik
goddesses (yoginis).

● **168**
Nava-graha (nine planets)
pataka, Rajasthan, 18th
century. Propitiation of the
nine planets, viz. Sun, Moon,
Mars, Mercury, Jupiter, Venus,
Saturn, Rahu (ascending node)
and Ketu (descending node) is
common all over India.

● **169**
Devi pataka worshipped
by the Jains, Rajasthan,
18th century.

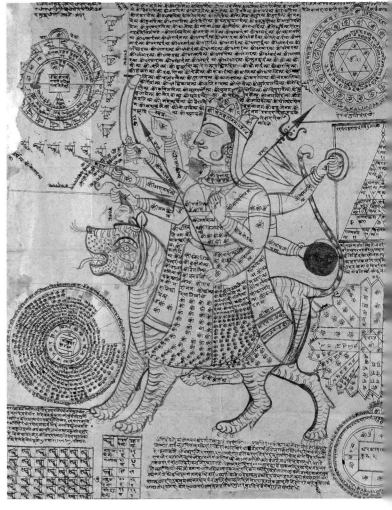

170
Bhairava pataka,
Rajasthan, 18th century.
Four-armed god, the ferocious
aspect of Shiva, is shown
standing on his mount, the
dog. Curiously, his body is
composed of a cosmic diagram,
inscribed with magical
formulae (mantras). Numerical
(anka) diagram (yantra) is seen
in the foreground.

171
A diagram (yantra) sacred to the Kaula tantriks, popularly known as the leftists (vama-margis). The leftist here does not have political connotations. Rajasthan, 17th century.

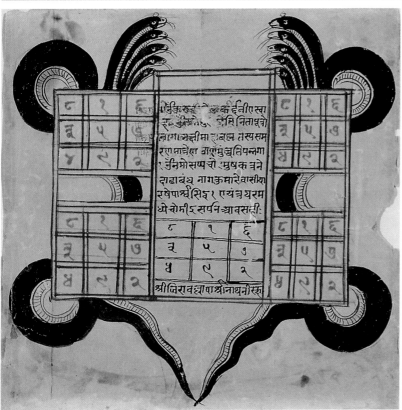

172
Nagavali yantra sacred to the Jain Tirthankar Parshvanath, Rajasthan, 18th century.

● **173**
An impressive portrayal of
Virabhadra, ferocious aspect
of Shiva, accompanied by his
dog vehicle. Karnataka;
19th century.

● **174**
Square cosmic diagram
(mandala) of a Shiva temple,
Rajasthan. 18th century.

● **175**
Goddess Hoi or Ahoi, painted on kite paper with vegetable colours, Kumaun hills, Uttaranchal, 19th century. A week before Diwali, festival of lights, celebrated in October-November every year, the housewives paint such images of the goddess for the well-being of their offspring. This painting is a unique example, the only one of its kind. This tradition prevails all over north India, upto Bihar, where the goddess is addressed as Syahu Mata. The mudwall paintings, floor decorations, clay toys and pottery and such like artifacts are the prerogatives of housewives who observe fasts and pray for their families' well-being. These craft traditions, like embroideries, have been nurtured by women all over India.

● 176–177
Episodes from the
Mahabharata, Paithan,
Maharashtra; 19th century.

● 178
A pictorial rendition of the
symbolism inherent in the
Primal sound as the
monosyllabic magic formula
(mantra) AUM, comprising all
the three prominent gods of
the Hindu pantheon: Brahma,
Vishnu and Mahesh (Shiva).
Kashmir; early 19th century.
Gouache on paper.

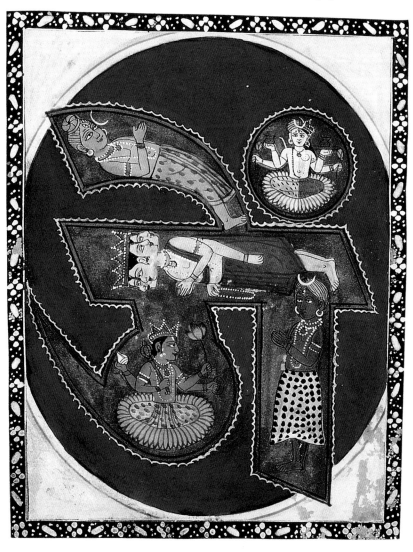

PAINTINGS – PATAKAS, TANTRIK AND FOLK

● **179**
Shiva and Parvati with a
royal attendant,
Jodhpur, Rajasthan;
early 19th century.

● **179**
Shiva and Parvati with a
royal attendant,
Jodhpur, Rajasthan;
early 19th century.

● **180**
A king enjoying a dance
performance, Mewar,
Rajasthan; 18th century.
A masterly capturing of the
palace scene by a rural artist.

K.C. ARYAN'S HOME OF FOLK ART

● **181**
A woman waiting at her
home entrance, Mewar,
Rajasthan; 18th century.

● **182**
Krishna the Divine Flute Player
enchanting one and all with his
magical notes, Mewar,
Rajasthan; 18th century.

● **183**
Hanuman with a chunk of a
mountain containing medicinal
herbs. Basohli; 18th century.

● **184**
A wood cut print of Goddess
Kali, Bengal; late 19th century.

PAINTINGS – PATAKAS, TANTRIK AND FOLK

● **185**
A wood cut print of five-
headed Shiva. Lord of music.
Bengal; late 19th century.

● 186
Hanuman flying over the
ocean to Lanka, Bengal;
19th century.

● **187**
Radha, Krishna with milkmaids standing under a tree. Pata painting; Bengal; late 19th century.

● **188–189**
Scroll painting or patachitra illustrating diverse stories; Bengal; late 19th century.

● **190**
Sahib (British soldiers) pata,
Bengal, late 19th century.

● **191**
Hanuman tearing open his
chest to show his genuine
devotion for Shri Rama.
Kalighat, 20th century.

● **192–193**
Birds and animals:
two illustrations from a
manuscript on omens
and prognostics. Gujarat;
19th century.

K.C. ARYAN'S HOME OF FOLK ART

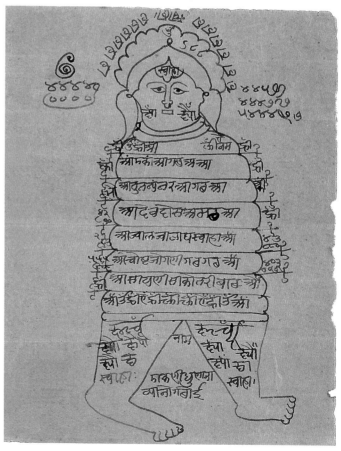

● 194
The Dakini Yantra, Rajasthan;
19th century.

● **195–196**
Shiva and Parvati, the epitome of conjugal bliss. Jodhpur, Rajasthan; 19th (top) and 18th (bottom) century.

● **197**
Hanuman searching medicinal
herbs. Mewar, Rajasthan;
17th century.

● **198**
Krishna looks on, while
foster-mother Yashoda churns
butter. Mewar, Rajasthan;
17th century.

199
Portrayal of Gomukh Yakshraj,
a winged fairy flying above
with garlands. Rajasthan;
19th century.

● **200**
Ganesh flanked by consorts Riddhi
and Siddhi (painting on fabric).
Rajasthan; 19th century.

a

b

● **201–202** *opposite*
Two folios from Jain
manuscript Sangrehanisutra
featuring (a) eight auspicious
symbols sacred to Jainism;
(b) double-headed eagle with
wide-spread wings. Rajasthan;
16–17th century.

● **203–204**
Folios from Sangrehanisutra
by Bhojdev, illustrating
(203) pipe players;
(204) drum (mridangam)
players; Kamadhenu
the celestial cow;
a seated figure and Ravana.
Rajasthan; 16th century.

204

203

● **205–214**
Folios illustrating scenes from
hell from a Jain manuscript.
Rajasthan. 16th-17th century.
Such paintings were intended
to instil the idea of a good
moral character in the viewers,
their themes being severe
punishments inflicted in hell
on evil-doers.

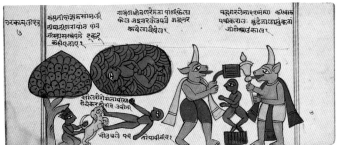

● 207–208

● 211

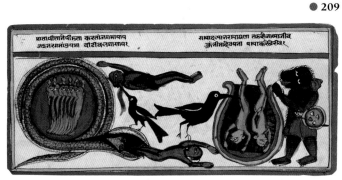

● 209

● 212

● 213

● 210

● 214

215
Folio from a Jain manuscript forewarning evil doers of the duration of their sojourn in hell. Rajasthan; 17th century.

216
Punishments for evil doers; a folio from a Jain manuscript. Gujarat. 17th century.

Folio illustrating scenes from
hell from a Jain manuscript -
punishments being meted out
to perpetrators of evil deeds.
Sirohi, Rajasthan; 16th century

PAINTINGS – PATAKAS, TANTRIK AND FOLK

● **218–221**
Folios illustrating scenes
from hell from a Jain
manuscript – punishments
being meted out to
perpetrators of evil deeds.
Sirohi, Rajasthan;
16th century

● **222** *opposite*
The seven infernal regions
(narakas). W. India.
18th century.

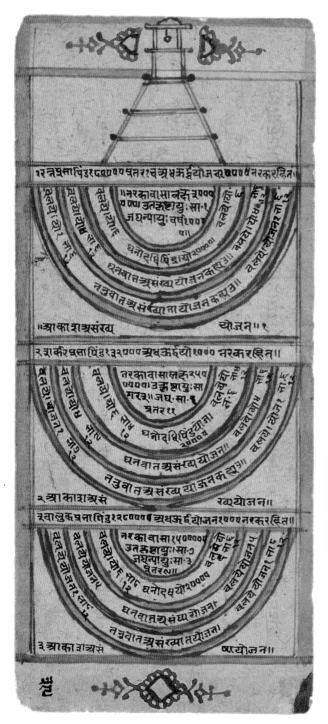

● 222

● 223
Narasimha, incarnation of
Vishnu killing demon
Hiranyakashipu, flanked by his
devotee Prahlad, Brahma and
Narada Muni, an illumination
from the Bhagvata Purana.
Jammu; 19th century.

● 224
Vasudeva carrying newly-born
Krishna across the river
Yamuna to Nanda's village.
Jammu. 19th century.

● 225
Worship of Vishnu enshrined
in a temple, Rajasthan;
19th century.

K.C. Aryan did for popular paintings of Punjab what W.G. Archer had done for those from Bengal, Bihar and Orissa. He was the only one who collected folk paintings and bazar school paintings from Punjab, especially Amritsar. These paintings were executed by both Hindu and Sikh artists. The themes are puranic by and large, although non-religious themes were also attempted. The treatment is conventional, but the style underwent a drastic change. Aniline dyes are used, instead of vegetable ones. This accounts for the lack of lyrical and rhythmic grace, fluency of line and soothing effects.

It needs to be stressed that these paintings and lithographs can be seen only in the collection of Home of Folk Art, and nowhere else. They are being reproduced for the first time.

● **226**
Shiva and Parvati filtering hemp (bhang), Litho print, Amritsar, Punjab; late 19th century.

● **227**
Vibrant portrait of Maharaja
Ranjit Singh on horseback,
with an attendant. Bazaar
school, Amritsar; 19th
century.

● **228**
Litho print: a train and British
soldiers. Amritsar, Punjab; late
19th century.

● **229**
A Nihang sikh churning
hemp. Bazaar school,
Amritsar. 19th century.

230

●230–233
Anantshayana Vishnu with
Lakshmi (230); Hanuman
leading the horse-drawn
chariot of Rama and Sita (231);
Laila Majnun (232); Heer
Ranjha, the famous lovers of
Punjab (233). Bazaar school,
Amritsar; 19th century.

231

232

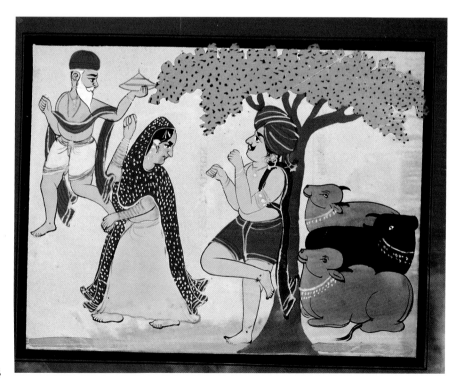

233

234

● **234–238**
The Hindu Trinity: Brahma, Vishnu and Mahesh (234); Narasimha Avatara of Vishnu (235); Shiva and Parvati, Nandi seated in foreground (236); composition of Ram mantra (237); Durga Mahishasuramardini (238). Bazaar school, Amritsar; 19th century. Of these No. 234 is a masterpiece in the sense that it still retains the strong pahari stylistic flavour in its overall treatment.

235

K.C. ARYAN'S HOME OF FOLK ART

236

237

238

● 239
Baby Krishna sucking the
breasts of demoness Putana,
a manuscript in Gurumukhi
script, Jammu, 19th century.

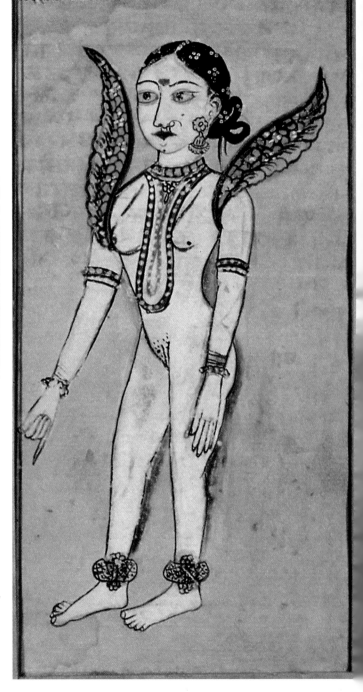

● 240
A winged fairy,
Jodhpur; 19th century.

● **241–242**
Puranic themes painted on the
accounts books (bahis)
maintained by the mercantile
community. Maharashtra;
19th century.

● **243**
Surya the Sun-god riding his
seven-horse-drawn chariot.
Gujarat; 17th-18th century.

● **245**
Five-headed Hanuman seated
in the posture of meditation
(padmasana) on a composite
animal, a crocodile with a fish's
tail. Kangra; 19th century.

● **244**
Hanuman paying obeisance
to his lord Rama, whose
younger brother Lakshman
is seen standing alongside.
Alwar school, Rajasthan.
19th century.

● **248**
Ganesh and Narasimha-
avatar of Vishnu flanked
by Prahlad and his
mother. Paper-cuts,
Mathura; 20th century.
This tradition dates from
the pre-Christian period.

● **246** *opposite*
Hanuman receiving blessings
from his lord Rama, standing
with brother Lakshman and
wife Sita. Mewar; 17th century.

● **247** *opposite*
Three women standing on the
terrace of a royal palace within
a fortress guarded by a
securityman. Mewar, 19th
century.

● **249**
Portrait of Bisal (Vishal) Dev,
a deified rural warrior.
Jodhpur, mid-18th century.

● **250**
Hanuman the singer and
musician (glass painting),
Western India. 19th century.

● **251**
Nine forms of Shri Nathji
(Lord Krishna). An unusual
torana (entrance decoration),
Nathdwara, Rajasthan.
19th century

K.C. ARYAN'S HOME OF FOLK ART

Book Covers

An Englishman on horse back and a man with a camel. Painted papier-mache bookcovers. Basohli or Bilaspur, H.P. 19th century.

● 254–255 *opposite*
Embroidered bookcovers featuring auspicious symbols sacred to the Jains. Gujarat; 19th century.

● **256**
Painted papier-mache
bookcover ornately decorated
with delicate floral designs.
Rajasthan, 19th century.

● **257**
Hanuman paying obeisance to
Rama and Sita. Painted
wooden manuscript cover
called *patia*, Bikaner, Rajasthan.
19th century.

Metalcraft

Lamps
Hemp Filters
Yantras
Jewellery
&
Other Objects

● **259**
Deep-lakshmi (metal oil
lamp). Orissa. 19th century.
H. 19.5 cm.

● **258**
Deep-lakshmi (metal oil lamp).
Orissa. 19th century.
H. 42 cm.

● **260**
Oil lamp for worship
(metal), Bengal;
19th century. H. 31 cm.

● 261–263
Oil lamps (iron),
Madhya Pradesh; 20th century.
H. 48 cm; 50 cm. & 43 cm.

● 265–267
Hemp filters (iron), Jodhpur;
20th century. The depiction of
Shiva lingam is on account of
the popular belief stressing
Shiva's fondness for hemp.
H. 52 cm; 21 cm & 36 cm.

● 264
Oil lamp with multiple
wicks used for temple
worship.
Nepal, 19th century.
H. 19 cms.

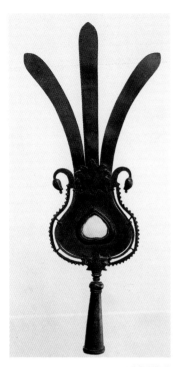

268–270
Alam, muslim standards
(metal), Lucknow;
late 19th century.
H. 60 cm; 32 cm & 37 cm.

271
Standard emblem portraying
the Moon God, legendary
progenitor of the Rajputs.
Rajasthan; 19th century.
D. 36 cm.

272
Salver portraying the Sun God
in the centre, the zodiac signs
and the twenty-seven planets
(Nakshatras). Jaipur. 19th
century. D. 61 cm.

273
A brass handfan engraved with
the Shiva-Lingam emblem for
ritualistic purpose. Rajasthan;
19th century. L. 17.5 cm

● **274**
The Panch Jina yantra.
Jain Siddha yantra for the
Nandishvara-dvipa worship.
Western India. 18th century.
L. 15 cm.

● **275**
The Mangala Yantra sacred to
Mars, portrayed in the centre,
engraved with magical
formulae (mantras). Rajasthan;
18th century. (Copper yantra
for worship). D. 22cm

● **276**
Eight auspicious
(ashtamangala) symbols sacred
to the Jains. (Brass yantra for
worship). Western India;
18th century. 8 x 8 cm.

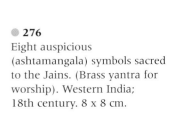

● **277–278**
Ritual brass pot decorated
with auspicious symbols and
Shri Yantra (copper).
Rajasthan. 18th century.
H. 9 cm. and 13.5 x 13.5 cm.

279
Silver ritual vessel engraved
with ten incarnations of
Vishnu. Rajasthan;
18th century. H. 20 cm.

280
Zoomorphic vessel (two-headed:
ram and boar with addorsed
bodies), brass, Rajasthan;
19th century. 15 x 10 cm.

281
Pre-Buddhist tribal deities
engraved on copper, Lahul-Spiti,
H. P.; 19th century. D. 25 cm.

282–284
Domestic utensils
(brass and iron)
(282) Madhya
Pradesh, H. 62 cm;
(283–84) Punjab;
H. 28 cm & 26 cm.
19th century.

● **285**
Silver crown for bridegroom engraved with Brahma, Ganesh and Vishnu; its other two components featuring Shiva and Durga are missing. Punjab and Himachal Pradesh; 19th century.

● **287**
Silver mouthpieces attached to the hubble-bubble (hukka) pipe used by aristrocrats. North India; 18th century.

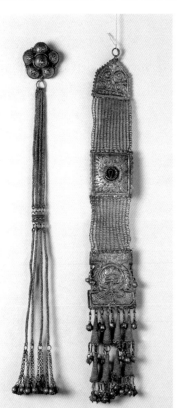

● **286**
Silver head ornaments, Kulu, H.P.; 18th century.

● **289**
A purse and a beaded ornament of the Gaddis of Chamba, H.P. 19th century.

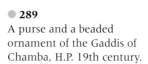

● **288**
Finial showing a dragon.

● **290**
A silver torque worn by tribals. Rajasthan and Madhya Pradesh; 19th century.

291
Ganga Sagar, Punjab, 19th century. A brass vessel for storing water with impressively designed handle and spout.
H. 30 cm.

292
Peacock motif surmounting an iron finial; a protective device placed on the rooftops of residential houses. Kulu, Himachal; contemporary.
H. 36 cm.

293
Traditional lock with two keys (iron), Punjab.
19th century. 17 x 14 cm.

294
Traditional locks (iron), called shanang in Kinnaur, Himachal, 19th century.
L. 15 cm; & 17.5 cm.

METALCRAFT

295
Mango and bird-shaped brass
vermilion containers in dhokra
technique. Bengal.
19th century. H. approx. 10 cm.

296
Bronze image of a bull with
wheels, Rajasthan.
19th century. H. 17cm.

297
A chariot.Rajasthan,
19th century. 29 x 19 cm.

298
A horse-driven chariot.
Rajasthan, 19th century.
26 x 20 cm. Such toys were
given to Rajput children to
instil war-like qualities in them
from early age.

299
Artistically designed brass
elbow-rest; central India.
19th century. Intended for a
meditating saint, it enabled him
to rest his elbow. H. 13 cm.

300
Brass combs. Bastar.
20th century.

301
Brass mask of Daksha, Shiva's
father-in-law. South India.
19th century. H. 37.5 cm.

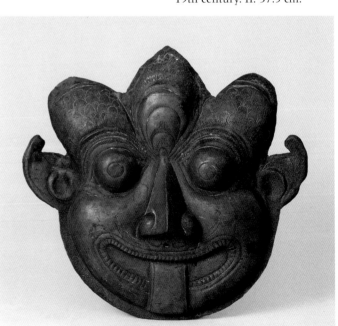

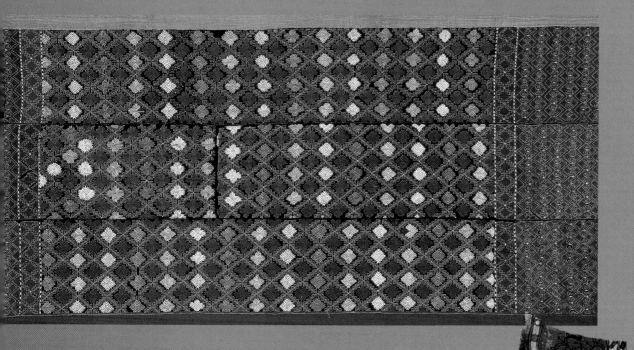

Textiles

Phulkaris
Pahari Rumals
Cholis
Kanthas
Gujarat Embroideries

TEXTILES

The museum has a vast collection of some of the best and most fascinating embroideries and appliques from the Punjab, Himachal Pradesh, Haryana, Uttar Pradesh, Bengal, Bihar, and Swat valley. They give us an insight into the lives of their makers, in most cases, rural housewives, unlettered women, young and old alike. They celebrate the vibrancy and creativity of rural women, and register their responses to their environs and societal changes through their textiles and costumes.

Embroideries and appliqued fabrics were intended for personal and family use, and embody a well-understood language of social identity and reflect the rural women's worldviews as well as values. The cultural context and meanings of what these splendid pieces meant to their creators and their family members are not difficult to grasp. The visual language was widely understood by members of diverse communities. The vocabulary of diverse embroidery styles from all over India highlights both their cultural diversity as well as homogeneity. Embroidery stitches, designs and motifs are more or less universal.
The richly hued veils bathed in shimmering golden yellows, greens, reds and blues from the phulkaris of Punjab, the pictorial rumals, embroidered on both the sides, wall hangings, caps, diceboards, women's bodices (cholis) from

Himachal Pradesh, kanthas from Bengal, a large variety of embroideries from Sind and Gujarat, and lesser known Swat embroideries are the glory of the museum collection, each piece selected with the discerning eye of an artist by late Mr. K.C.Aryan.

PHULKARIS AND BAGH

'Phulkari' means 'flower work' and bagh is 'garden'. In the rural and urban Punjab, as everywhere else in India, women, young and old alike, living in tradition-bound families, have to keep their heads covered with an odhani (veil). For this purpose, a large piece of coarse cotton fabric, khaddar, invariably terracotta red, sometimes black and rarely white, about two metres in length and one metre broad, embroidered in variegated coloured silk threads in a variety of designs.

Phulkari is not a simple veil; on it are embroidered the semiological patterns of the discourse of her cultural destiny. It is a small world where nature is not very distant from culture. The conceptual distances are created by the abstract forms of multicoloured squares and circles, impressionistic configurations and the composite blend of all the symbols required for a proportional, harmonious setting of a carefully worked out meditation system. In its extreme simplicity lies its sublimity. The brightness of

colours and the parallelism of forms are definitely high watermarks of aesthetics but it would indeed be extremely misleading if one did not concentrate on the significance of these marvellous designs. It is certainly not an affair of an assemblage of superstitions, but a highly complicated abstract network of symbols due to steady growth of well-tuned mind and a vision beautiful and incisive.

Phulkaris and baghs were embroidered in Peshawar, Rawalpindi, Hazara, Chakwal, Jhelum and Sialkot in West Punjab (modern Pakistan), and Amritsar, Jullundhar, Kapurthala, Patiala, Hoshiarpur, Ludhiana, Ferozpur and Bhatinda in east Punjab.

THE SWAT EMBROIDERIES

The museum has an excellent collection of fascinating embroideries from the North-western Frontier Provinces, especially Swat. The traditional embroidery is done on the costumes, especially women's costumes such as the upper garment (jumlo), shawl used for covering the head, coverlets, pillow covers etc. For all these articles, black or blue-black coarse handspun cotton is used on which elaborate embroidery is done with floss silk threads, but the range of colours is minimal. Magenta or deep pink is the predominant colour. These shades contribute to the overall sombre effect.

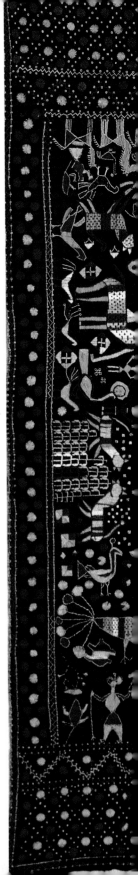

● **302–303**
Figural phulkaris (embroidered
veils for women), East Punjab;
19th century.

304

305

K.C. ARYAN'S HOME OF FOLK ART

● **304–306**

Darshan Dwar Phulkaris, East
Punjab; 19th century. Shrines
with slanting roofs enclosing
human figures are depicted on
terracotta red ground in two
rows. Peacocks and floral
motifs common to phulkaris
are added in contrasting
colours, white, purple, yellow,
blue, green or pale pink.

306

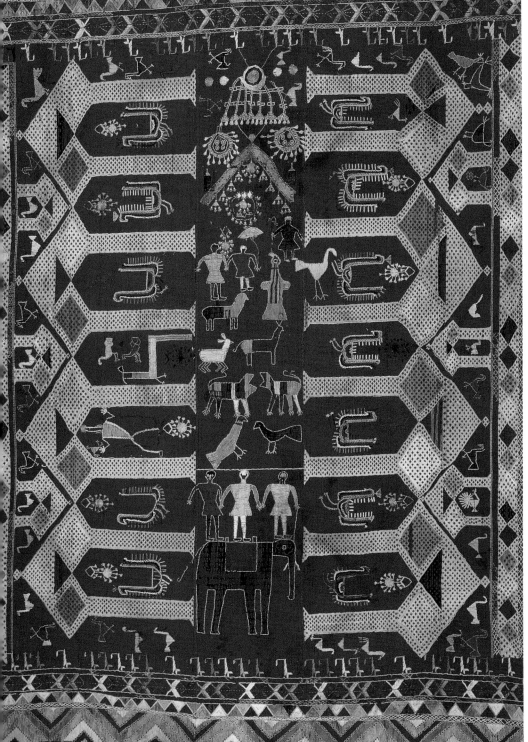

● **307–309**
Darshan Dwar Phulkaris, East
Punjab; 19th century. In fig.
309 a train motif is deftly
integrated.

K.C. ARYAN'S HOME OF FOLK ART

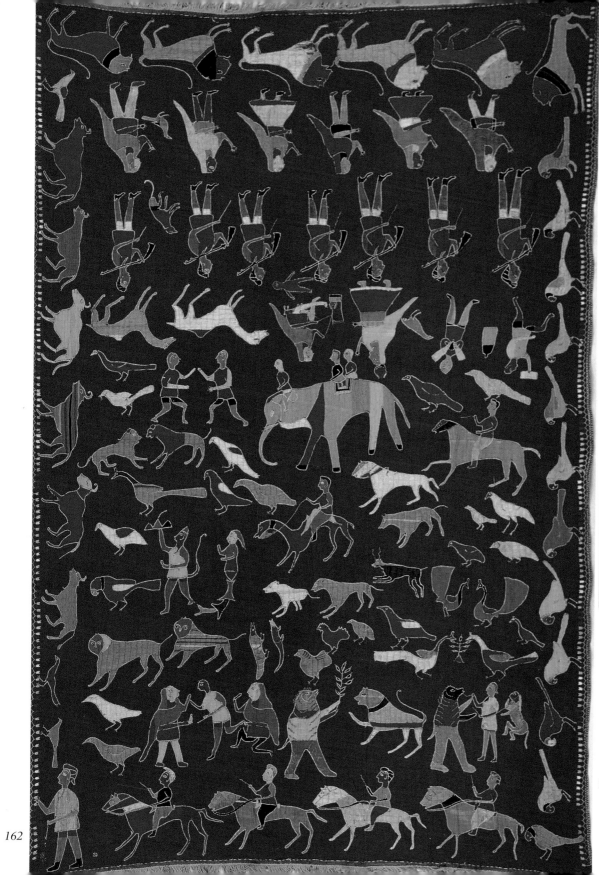

162

310

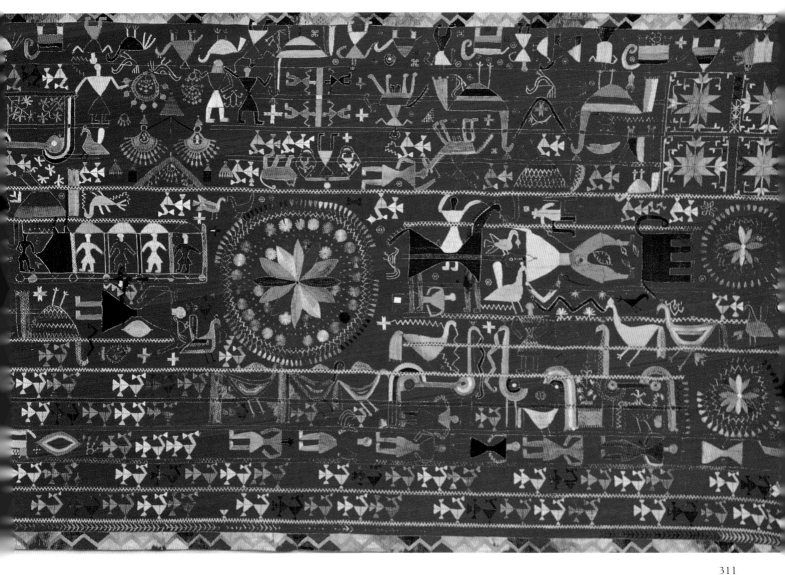

● 310–311
Sainchi phulkari, east Punjab;
19th century. Coarse cotton
embroidered with bright red,
golden yellow, blue and green
silk threads on terracotta red
ground. White and black cotton
threads are used. The motifs
are all drawn from life around.

TEXTILES: PHULKARIS

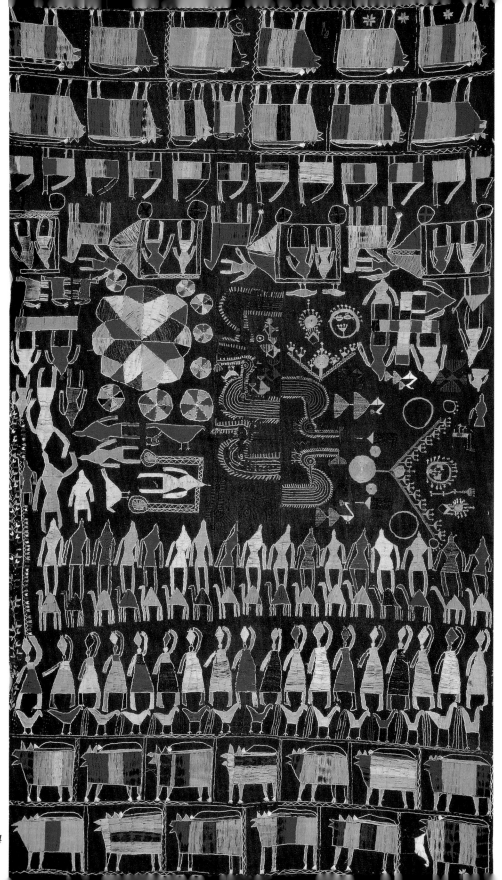

● **312–313**
Sainchi phulkaris. East Punjab;
19th century. On black cotton
khaddar, motifs such as human
figures, birds, animals, a
woman's personal ornaments,
floral designs, stylised peacocks
(a favourite motif) are
embroidered in a baffling
variety.

K.C. ARYAN'S HOME OF FOLK ART

313

● **314–315**
Sainchi phulkaris. East Punjab; 19th century. On black cotton khaddar, motifs such as human figures, birds, animals, a woman's personal ornaments, floral designs, stylised peacocks (a favourite motif) are embroidered in a baffling variety.

314

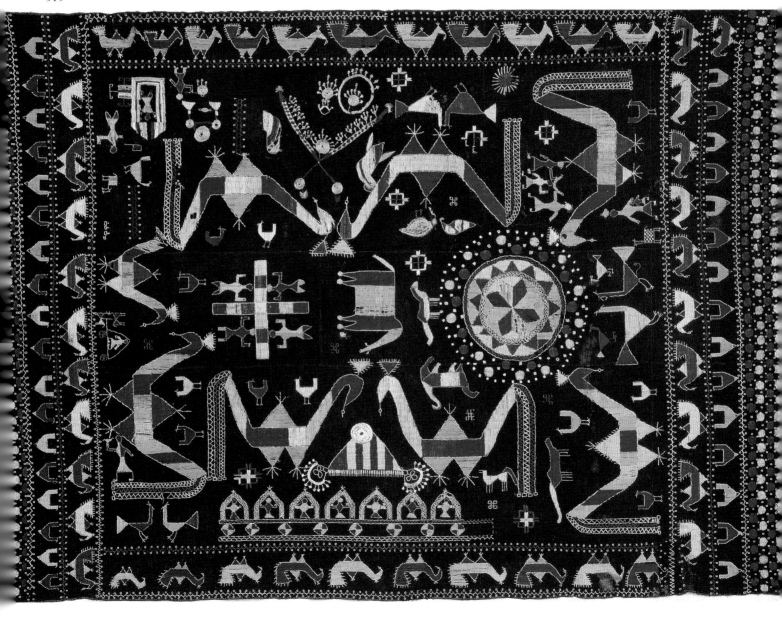

TEXTILES: PHULKARIS

167

● 316
The Bawan Bagh, an album of
fifty-two motifs. East Punjab;
19th century.

● 317
Chope phulkari, east Punjab;
19th century. Superb play of
imagination with golden yellow
silk threads on terracotta red
ground.

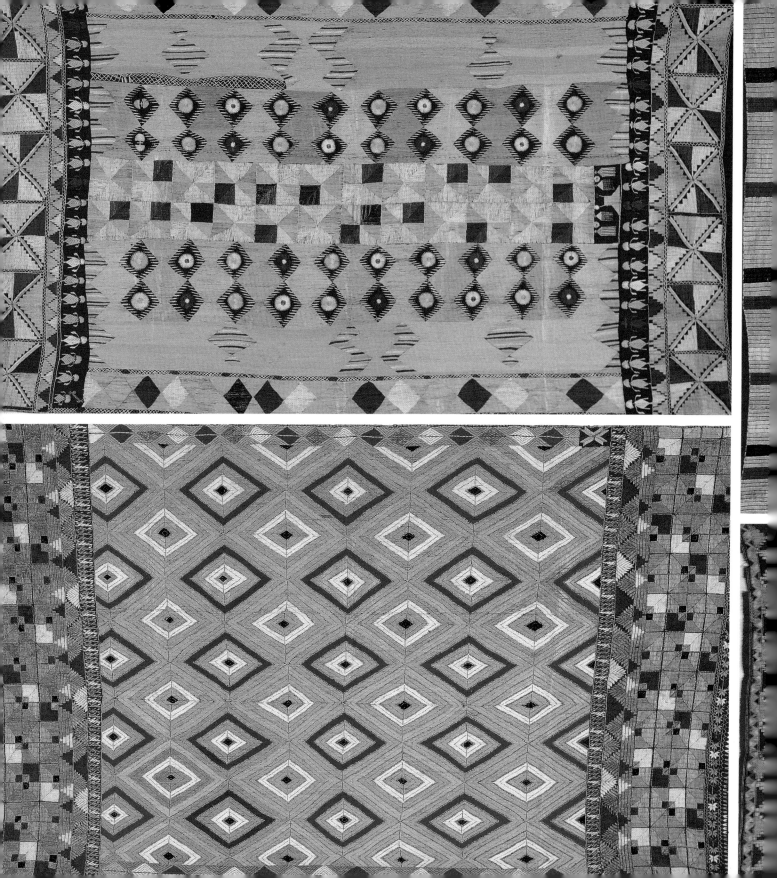

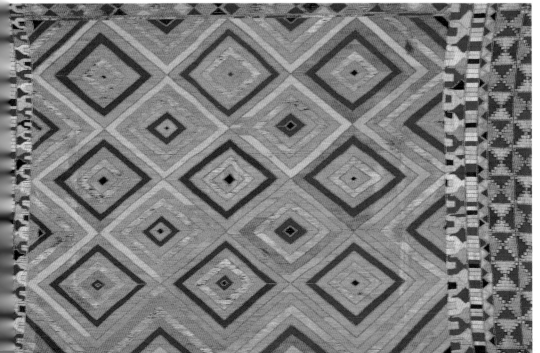

● **318–321**
Bagh, east Punjab; 19th
century. When the brick red
fabric is entirely covered with
designs worked with silk
threads, it is called bagh
(a garden full of flowers), or
vari-da-bagh (phulkari
intended for the bride
embroidered by groom's
mother or grandmother).
Shimmering yellow silk threads
are harmoniously combined
with white, green and blue.

322
Asharfi bagh, east Punjab;
19th century. Circular motifs
are asharfis (gold or silver
coins) embroidered in deep
pink, white and pale green on
golden-yellow silk threads that
cover the entire surface.

● **323**
A highly impressive bagh,
east Punjab; 19th century.

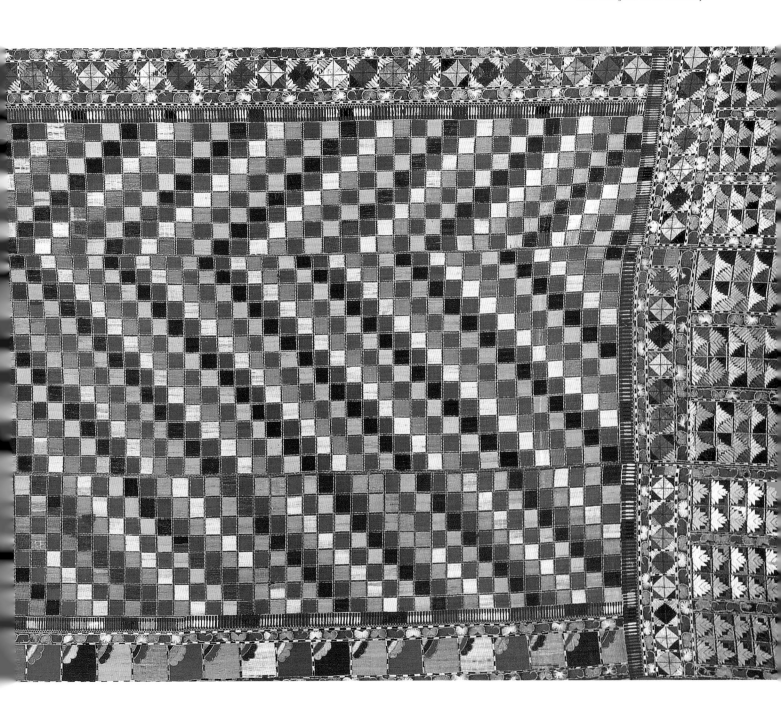

TEXTILES: PHULKARIS

324

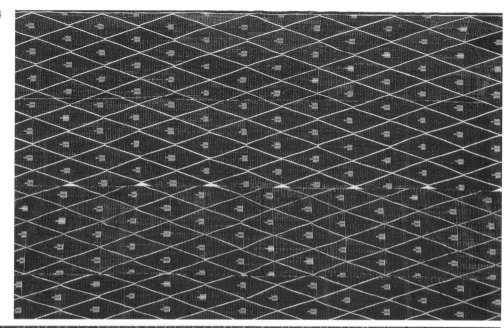

● 324–327

Baghs from Rawalpindi, West
Punjab; 19th century. On white
cotton fabric, attractive designs
formed by criss-cross lines,
diamond-shapes, zigzag
patterns etc. are embroidered
with purplish pink silk threads.
The effect is very pleasing.
Notable is the contrast in
colour schemes.

325

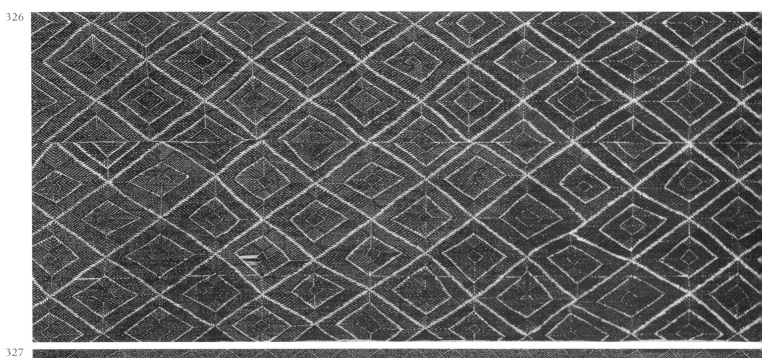

326

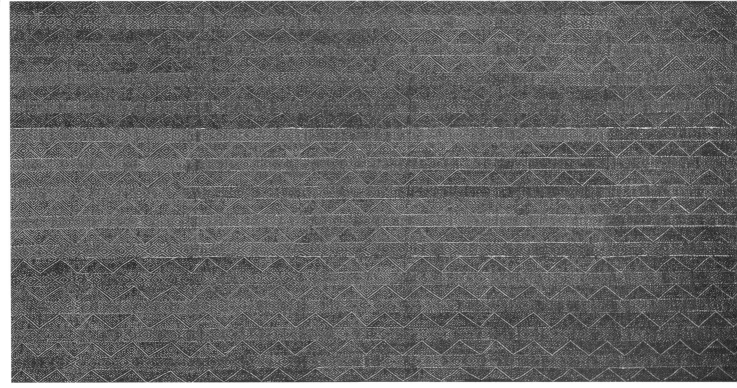

327

● **328**
Chand Phulkari, Hazara (now in Pakistan) 19th century. Unlettered rural women's perception of and fascination with the moon finds expression in this phulkari, the entire surface of which is covered with this silvery motif. The lateral ends provide a lively contrast, embroidered in golden yellows and deep oranges.

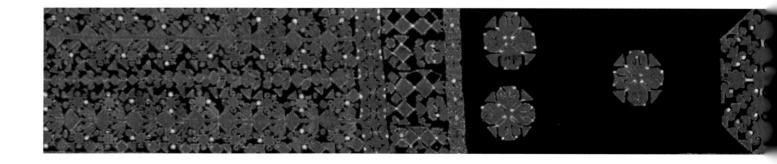

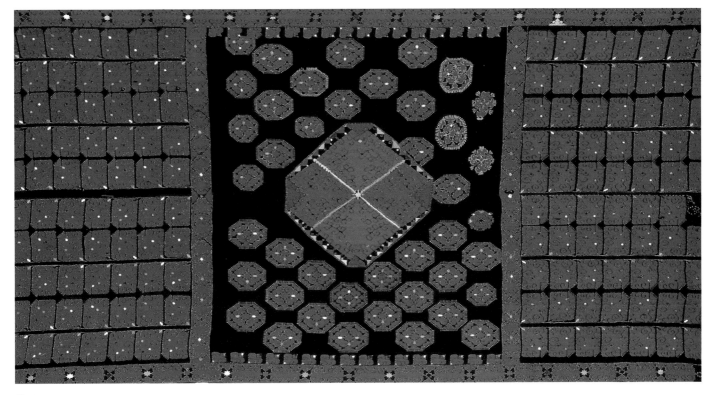

329
Embroidered shawl. Swat valley (Pakistan); 20th century. On black cotton surface, stylised floral patterns akin to the phulkaris of Punjab are embroidered by rural housewives of Swat.

330
Embroidered wedding turban. Swat valley; 20th century. Lavishly embroidered turban used by men display the same geometric patterns as seen on the shawls for women.

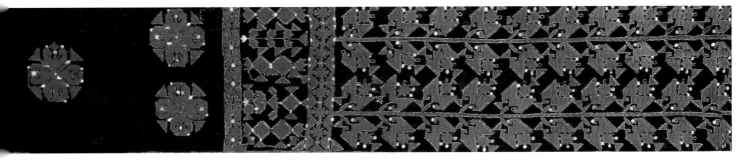

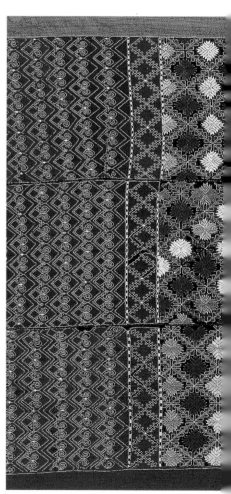

● **331**
Embroidered shawl. Swat valley;
20th century.

Embroidered shawl. Swat
valley; 20th century. Slight
change in colour schemes is
discernible here. Floral designs
embroidered in white and
green are sprinkled evenly on
the inner space.

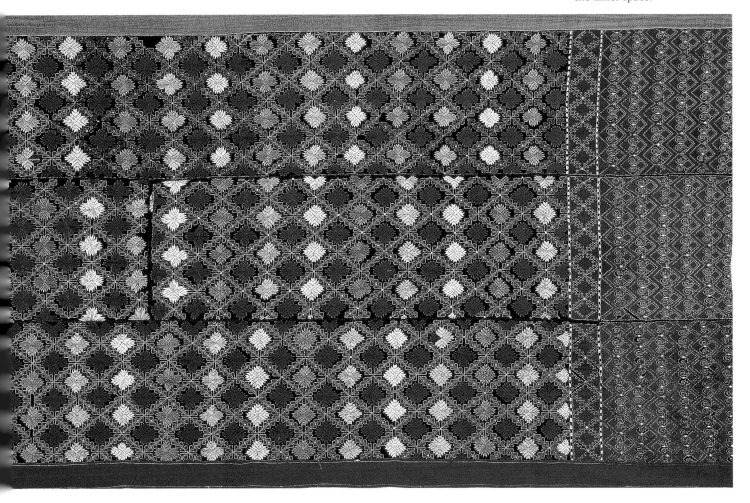

333
Square coverlet, Swat valley;
20th century. This embroidered
cotton coverlet like the
Himachal rumals shows a
central square mandala, and
plants in the corners pointing
towards it. Yellows and greens
added to deep pink enliven its
pleasing effect.

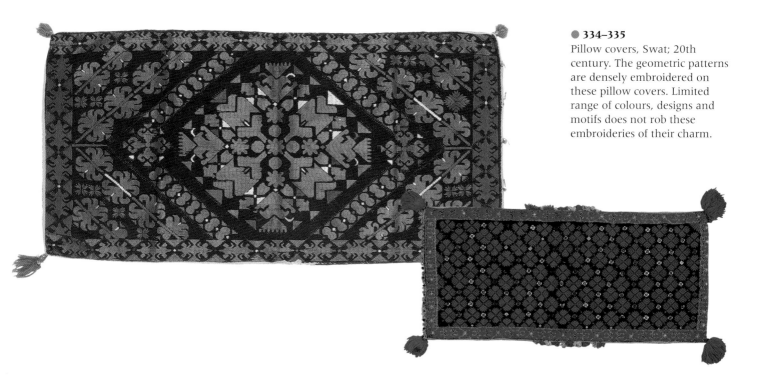

334–335
Pillow covers, Swat; 20th
century. The geometric patterns
are densely embroidered on
these pillow covers. Limited
range of colours, designs and
motifs does not rob these
embroideries of their charm.

PICTORIAL EMBROIDERIES FROM HIMACHAL PRADESH

The state of Himachal Pradesh stands out from the rest of the country for the enchanting style of embroidery evolved by its housewives. Popularly known as rumals, they are embroidered on both the sides by using double satin stitch, using extremely fine transparent muslin. Examples earlier than the 18th century are not available. In earliest rumals, silk threads dyed in vegetable colours were used; these distinguish them from later rumals, embroidered on opaque muslin using bright, almost garish silk threads. Rumals were embroidered in Chamba, Kangra, Mandi, Nurpur and Bilaspur, but not elsewhere. Wall hangings, cholis (blouses), caps, dice-boards, coverlets and sashes were also embroidered, but they are not reversible.

● **336**
Flute-playing Krishna flanked by milkmaids (gopis): Chamba, 18th century. The fine muslin ground and use of soft colours obtained from vegetable dyes differentiate early rumals from later ones.

● **337**
The rasa dance of Krishna and gopis around Ganesha seated in the centre. Chamba; 19th century.

● 338
Embroidered floral and geometric designs on black cotton fabric. Nurpur; 20th century. This rumal was collected from Nurpur from a Hindu household; its striking affinities with Swat embroideries indicate that its embroiderer hailed from Swat valley and was married to a native.

● 339
Hanuman embroidered skilfully on a cotton wall hanging. The woman embroiderer did not wish to remain anonymous. Her name Sarla Kumari figures along with the opening couplet of Hanuman Chalisa.
20th century.

● 340
Ganesh with a female attendant and elephant riders. Embroidered rumal, Chamba, 19th century.

● 341
Radha and Krishna flank the lotus rosette. Chamba, 19th century.

● 342
Marriage of Krishna and Rukmini being solemnised in a mandapa (vedi). Kangra, 19th century.

● 343
Adoration of Ganesha seated on a lotus cushion. Kangra, 19th century.

340

341

342

343

TEXTILES: PAHARI RUMALS

● **344**
Ganesh in the inner
mandala surrounded by
female figures
worshipping the sacred
Tulsi plant. Kangra,
19th century.

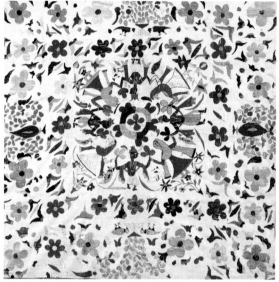

● **345**
Krishna's rasa dance with the
milkmaids of Braja. Kangra,
19th century.

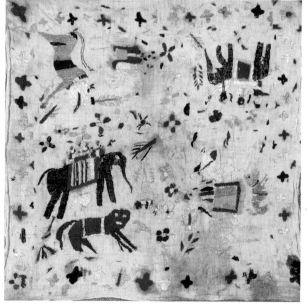

● **346**
Elephant-riders and
lions. Kangra, 19th
century.

● **347**
The Sun mandala and
Krishna's rasa dance.
Kangra, 19th century.

● **348**
A hanging portraying Ganesh
with devotees, a rare example
of devotional hymns in praise
of Ganesh embroidered all over
in Devanagari. Chamba,
19th century.

● 349
Ganesh surrounded by animal figures. Kangra, 19th century

350

351

352

● 350
The rasa dance of Krishna and gopis around a lotus mandala in the centre. Chamba; mid 18th century

● 351
Blue-bodied god Krishna draped in a yellow dhoti enthroned on a flat lotus seat and encircled by a highly impressive, colourful floral design, Kangra; mid 18th century.

● 352
Radha and Krishna. Kangra; 19th century. Bands of floral designs separate the Divine Lovers.

● 353
Horse and elephant riders. Kangra; 19th century. Very often, the rumal is divided into four parts, each depicting a motif, as in this example. These motifs are reminiscent of the days of Rajput pageantry.

● 354
Horse-riders, Radha and Krishna. Kangra, 19th century. Highly simplified forms of animals, human and divine figures, very similar to the figures painted on the mudwalls of rural homes, are impressive.

● 355–356
Lotus mandala with human figures. Bhadrawah-Kishtwar; 19th century. On black cotton fabric, embroidery is done in sombre shades of red, purple, pink, white and black, using chain stitches; the design is similar to that of Chamba rumals, but embroidery style is Kashmiri, evidently the work of a muslim gujjar woman.

356

● **357**
Krishna and Radha in a
palanquin, surrounded by
luscious flowers and dancing
peacocks. Bilaspur, 19th
century.

● **358**
(a) Krishna with milkmaids,
(b) Vishnu seated on a lotus
seat. Mandi; Himachal Pradesh.
19th century.

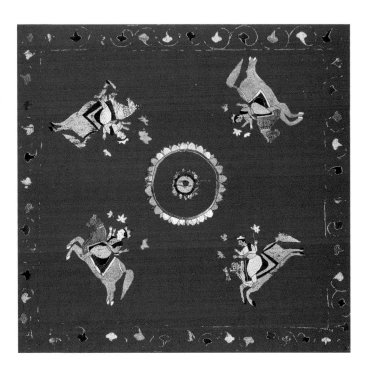

● 360
Prancing horseriders; Mandi; 19th century. Mandi is known for embroidery done on red cotton fabric, which differentiates it from the rest of Himachal Pradesh.

● 359
Floral designs interspersed with mirrors embroidered on a coverlet, Mandi; 19th century.

● 361
Rasalila and floral rosettes on coverlets. Mandi; Himachal Pradesh. 19th century.

● **362**
The Rasa dancers. Kangra,
late 19th century.

● **363**
Krishna dancing with gopis.
Nurpur (Kangra dist.) 19th
century. The simplified, archaic
forms of the Divine Flautist and
his companions seem to have
been inspired by the mudwall
paintings. The floral motifs are
similar to those of the phulkaris
from Punjab.

K.C. ARYAN'S HOME OF FOLK ART

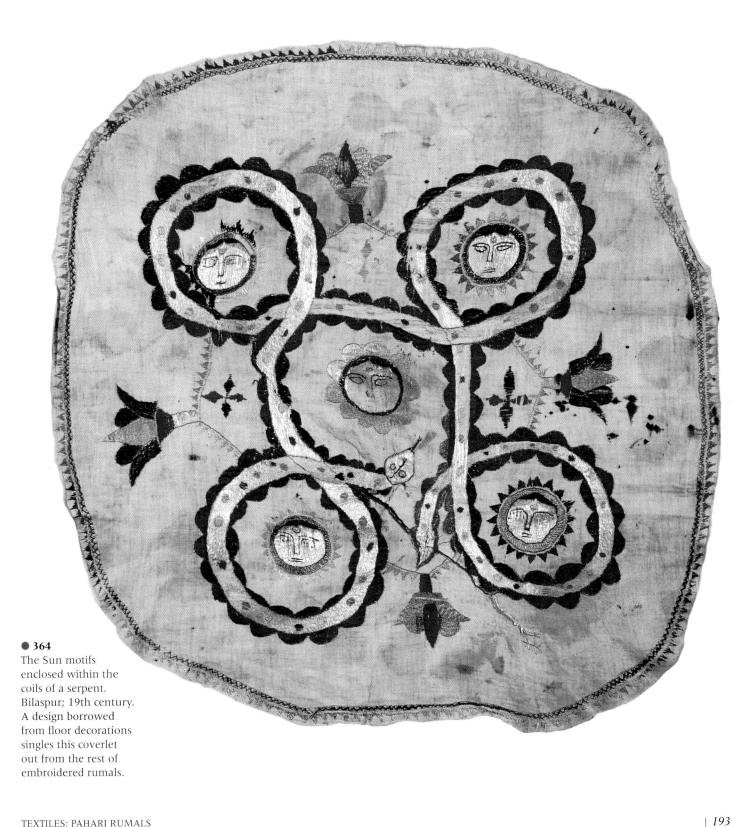

364
The Sun motifs
enclosed within the
coils of a serpent.
Bilaspur; 19th century.
A design borrowed
from floor decorations
singles this coverlet
out from the rest of
embroidered rumals.

TEXTILES: PAHARI RUMALS

● **365**
A wedding scene. Nurpur; 19th century. A common theme embroidered in rural flavour. The marriage mandapa (vedi) decorated with parrots encloses the figure of Brahma performing the wedding rites, while relatives and guests are seen all around.

● **366**
Krishna with gopis. Kangra; 19th century. In spite of the summary delineation of the figures, this rumal has a pleasing effect.

367
Bride's embroidered kurta. Punjab; 20th century. Lavishly embroidered silk kurta, worked with silk and gold-wrapped thread embroidery and metal spangles was intended to be worn by a bride at her betrothal and wedding ceremonies. This tradition was prevalent all over Punjab and Sind.

368-369
Embroidered backless bodices. Sind or Gujarat. 19th century.

370–371
Embroidered backless bodices
for women. North-western
region (now in Pakistan); 19th
century. Ornately embroidered
cotton bodices, decorated with
floral rosettes and small pieces
of mirror are worn by women
of nomadic tribes.

373
Embroidered bodice, Sind or Gujarat, 19th century. Densely embroidered floral designs on cotton base worked in chain stitch are common to cholis worn by Sindhi and Gujarati women.

372
Embroidered backless bodice; Sind; 20th century. Floral and peacock motifs are embroidered on this choli worn by girls from Lohana merchant's community in Sind.

374
Embroidered backless bodice, North-western region (now in Pakistan); 19th century.

375

Women's embroidered upper garment (jumlo or kurta). Swat valley; 20th century. The variety of designs embroidered in bright pink is amazing, ranging from scattered to dense geometric motifs. Bands of exceptionally fine embroidery at each shoulder are common to all examples.

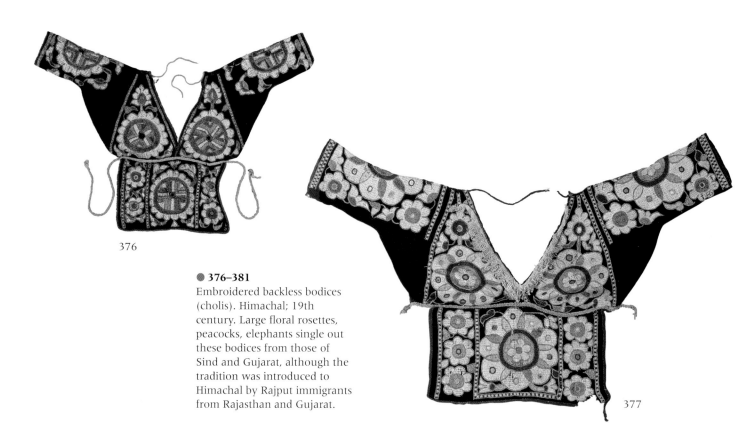

376

376–381

Embroidered backless bodices (cholis). Himachal; 19th century. Large floral rosettes, peacocks, elephants single out these bodices from those of Sind and Gujarat, although the tradition was introduced to Himachal by Rajput immigrants from Rajasthan and Gujarat.

377

378

379

380

381

382
Embroidered handfan featuring
a royal personnage with two
female attendants. Kangra;
19th century.

383
Embroidered cap ornamented
with lotus buds and a
meandering creeper. Chamba;
19th century.

384
Appliquéd cover (chadar or kanduri). Bahraich, Uttar Pradesh; 19th century. Such kanduris are offered to the shrine of Salar Masud, nephew of Mahmud Ghazni, at Bahraich. The depiction of Hindu legends indicates the syncretic character of his worship.

385
Appliquéd cover. South India; 19th century. Neatly divided into two parts, featuring Ganesh on his rat mount and Karttikeya on his peacock.

386–388

Embroidered kantha. Jessore (Bangladesh); 19th century. Quilts made of discarded cotton saris are embroidered with pleasing motifs, figural and floral. A large lotus mandala and floral sprays in the corners is the commonest theme.

386

387

388

389
Embroidered kantha featuring
elephant riders. Bangladesh;
19th century.

390
Embroidered kantha depicting
a large peacock with riders,
floral and mango motifs.
Bangladesh; 19th century.

Embroidered kantha showing
genre scenes around a lotus
mandala. Bangladesh;
19th century.

● **392–393** *opposite*
Embroidered kantha showing
elegant rosettes, paisleys,
peacocks around a lotus
mandala. Bangladesh;
19th century.

392

393

● **394**
Embroidered kantha.
Bangladesh; 20th century.
Scenes from everyday life as
perceived by a housewife –
a departure from the
traditional themes.

394

395 *opposite*
Embroidered kantha, Bangladesh; 19th century. A large lotus mandala in the centre and floral sprays – the usual features of this folk style embroidery – are combined with the women embroiderer's responses to real life incidents: a tiger walking away with its prey, a live woman; an Englishman astride his horse, while another sitting on a chair tortures a native whose mother protests in despair. A valuable visual documentation of contemporary events.

396
Embroidered kantha: a star shaped mandala surrounded by usual bird and animal motifs. Bangladesh; 19th century.

397
Kantha featuring an elephant. Bangladesh; 19th century.

● **398**
Appliquéd pennant of a standard. Haryana; 20th century. Such flags were used by Muslim followers of the Gugga cult on the Gugga Navami day in August. Gugga is shown astride a camel and the snake on top indicates his ability to cure people of snake-bite.

● **399**
Appliquéd square hanging (chakla). Gujarat; 19th century. Vishnu reclining on Anant serpent and Brahma perched on the lotus issuing from his navel is depicted deftly on this hanging.

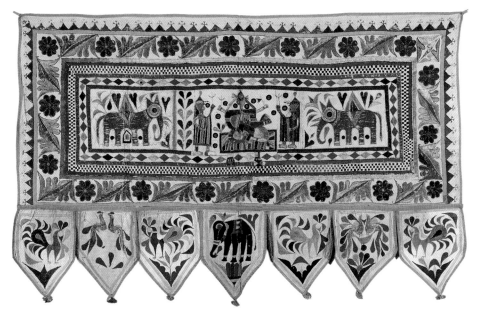

● **400**
Embroidered torana (frieze
hanging). Saurashtra, Gujarat;
19th century.

● **401**
Square appliquéd hanging
(chakla). Saurashtra, Gujarat;
19th century. Such hangings,
embroidered or appliquéd were
used in the absence of mudwall
paintings.

● **402**
Embroidered cover for a pile
of quilts. Saurashtra, Gujarat;
19th century. It shows
ingenious combination of
floral and geometric motifs,
embroidery and appliqué
technique.

403
Embroidered dice-board
(chaupar), Chamba, Himachal;
19th century.

404
Wedding shawl (woollen). Barmer,
Rajasthan; 19th century. White,
black and golden yellow cotton
threads are used for embroidering
geometric patterns on woollen
ground.

405
Dice-board made of beads.
Karnataka, 20th century.

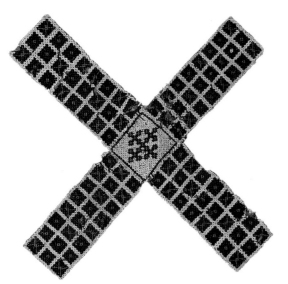

Woodcraft

● **406**
Krishna quelling the Kaliya serpent (Kaliyamardana). A wooden bracket from Kangra dwelling house, Himachal; 19th century. H. 54 cm.

● **407**
Mythical animal carved in wood, Ladakh. 20th century. L.61 cm.

● **408**
Wooden water spout shaped like a lion's head. Jubbal (Shimla hills), Himachal; 20th century. It is also used as a mask in the local dance-drama "Sih". L. 39 cm.

212

● **409**
Votive offering : a wooden panel featuring Ganesh, Himachal; early 18th century. H. 38 cm.

● **410–411**
Tribal woodcarvings. Bastar, Chhattisgarh; 20th century. H. 60 cm each.

● **412**
A striking tribal head. North-eastern India; 20th century.
H. 31 cm.

● **413**
Four-armed tribal goddess;
Himachal, 20th century.
H. 53 cm.

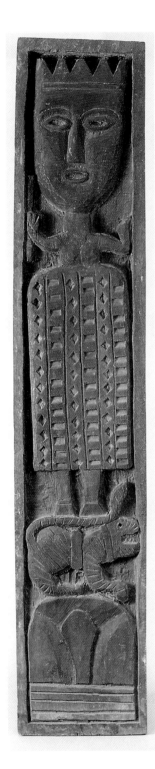

● **414–416**
Votive offerings : wooden panels carved with the figure of Durga. Shimla hills; Himachal; 20th century. Such panels are offered to the Devi on the fulfilment of vows and wishes. H. 114; 114; 112 cm.

417
Turban hanger (wood),
Gujarat; 19th century.
Ingeniously designed utilitarian
object, it features stylised horse
heads with long necks joined
together by intertwined ropes.
H. 54 cm.

418
Elephant and horse riders
(wood). Bastar, Chhattisgarh;
20th century. H. 92 cm.

419
A temple door guardian
(wood),Shimla hills, Himachal;
20th century. H. 78 cm.

● **420**
The Nagaraja (king of snakes), Kerala; 19th century. Such images are worshipped on the Naga Panchami festival in August. H. 38 cm.

● **422**
Wooden mask of a tribal hunter. North-eastern India; 20th century. H. 43 cm.

● **421**
The lion head (wood). South India; 19th century. It has striking affinities with stone statues of lions from South Indian temples as well as with traditional masks used in dance-dramas. H. 44 cm.

423

424

Wooden masks from Himachal
and Nepal. 19th century.
H. 30 cm; 28 cm; 27 cm and
32 cm.

425

426

● **427**
Painted mask of Hanuman
(papiermache), Orissa;
19th century. H. 35 cm.

● **428**
Wooden mask from tribal
areas of Himachal.
19th century. H. 29 cm.

● **429**
Tribal mask from Bastar.
20th century. H. 24 cm.

● **430**
Wooden mask from tribal
areas of Himachal.
20th century. H. 32 cm.

● **431–432**
Tribal painted wooden masks from Bastar, Chhattisgarh; 20th century. H. 36 cm & 40 cm.

● **433–434**
Wooden masks from Nepal (tribal), 19th century. H. 38 & 29 cm.

● **435 & 437**
Tribal wooden masks
from Himachal;
19th century.
H. 32 & 27 cm.

● **436**
Painted wooden mask. Bastar,
Chhattisgarh; 20th century.
H. 44 cm.

438
North-eastern tribal wooden mask, 20th century. H. 38 cm.

439
Wooden mask representing a king. Chamba, Himachal, 20th century. H. 46 cm.

440
A tribal goddess, Bastar, Chhattisgarh; 20th century. H. 200 cm.

● 442
Double-faced marriage
post (painted wood)
used by the Gond tribe,
Bastar, Chhattisgarh,
20th century. H. 175 cm.

● 441
Wooden statue of a tribal god,
Bastar, 20th century.
H. 139 cm.

● **443**
Genre scenes carved on a
wooden panel : a votive
offering; Shimla hills,
19th century. 40 x 34 cm.

● **444–445**
Carved wooden panels
featuring a drummer and
a devotee. Shimla hills;
20th century. H. 39 & 38 cm.

● **446**
Durga astride her lion mount
(wood), Shimla hills;
19th century. H. 28 cm.

● **447**
Painted cork statue of Gugga
Chauhan, Jodhpur, Rajasthan;
19th century. H. 31 cm.

● **448**
A lacquered wooden lid featuring renowned Marwar lovers Dhola-Maru on camelback. Jaisalmer, Rajasthan. 18th century.

● **449**
Wooden corks for lidding gun-powder containers. Jodhpur, 19th century. Their designs have been inspired by local architecture.

● **451**
Ganesh in wood, Gujarat.
19th century. H. 12 cm.

● **452**
Ghuggi, a wooden toy bird
(lacquered) with wheels.
Hoshiarpur, Punjab.
20th century.

● **450**
Wooden painted portable
shrine of Krishna (Jagannathji)
and his brother Balarama.
Rajasthan; late 18th century.
Their sister Subhadra's image is
missing. The trio are
worshipped most fervently in
their temple at Puri in Orissa.
H. 32 cm.

● **453**
Wooden painted flags
sacred to the Jains,
carved with fish and
eagle emblems.
Rajasthan.
19th century.

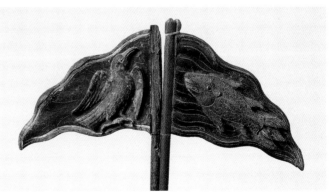

454
An ornately carved wooden
box. North India.
19th century. 23 x 10 cm.

● **455**
Wooden tribal combs, Bastar,
20th century. Such combs
carved by young boys are
offered to young girls whom
they propose to; if accepted,
they live together in a cottage
(gotul).

● **456**
A wooden musical instrument
similar to sarangi; Santhal
tribe; 20th century.
H. 93 cm.

● **457**
Painted wooden images of a
tribal couple. North-eastern
India. 20th century.

● **458**
A wooden box inlaid with
ivory. Rajasthan. 20th century.

Oleographs

● Oleographs from
Raja Ravi Varma press.

श्री छत्रपती शिवाजी महाराज.

● **459**
Shivaji on horseback marching
ahead; his fortress is seen in the
background.

● **460**
Lakshmibai, the famous Rani
(queen) of Jhansi, who fought
the British soldiers in the
uprising of 1857.

झाशीची राणी लक्ष्मीबाई.

SHREE MAHA RANAPRATAP

461-463
Maharana Pratap of Udaipur,
Rajasthan, who refused to yield
to the Mughal emperor Akbar.

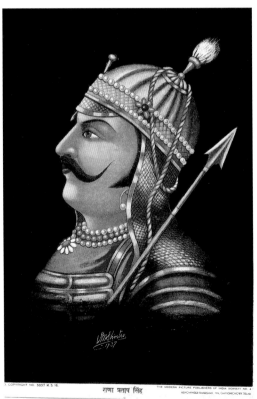

राणा प्रताप सिंह

राणा प्रताप सिंह

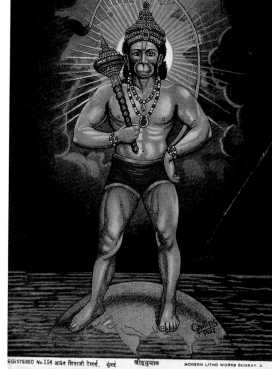

● 465
Krishna frolicking with
the bathing Gopis whose
garments he has stolen.

● 467
Portrait of Hanuman
with a muscular body,
befitting a warrior.

● 464
Ganesh with his consort
Riddhi, lithoprint of a
painting by Raja Ravi
Varma, 20th century.

● 466
Sarasvati seated on a lotus
throne playing on her veena,
accompanied by a swan and
a peacock.

468
Hanuman seated on his coiled
tail in front of Ravana in his
court in Lanka.

469
Vishwamitra refuses to accept
his daughter Shakuntala being
presented to him by Menaka.

● 470
Lakshmi.

● 471
Bharat Mata
(Mother India)

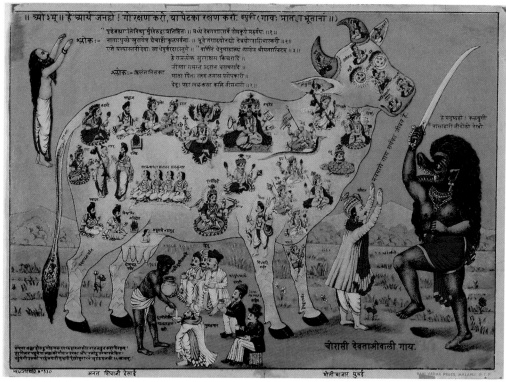

● 472
A propagandist print urging
Hindus to protect the sacred
cow.

AFTERWORD

India has the rare distinction of possessing continuing traditions of arts and crafts over five millennia. Few areas in the world can claim an art heritage comparable to that developed in India over the course of these millennia. But the artistic and cultural history of India, as recorded by the archaeologists and culture historians of our country, is for most part a history of the art of the urban aristocracy. What the world seems to have been oblivious of, at least till the recent past, was the inordinately rich and vibrant folk and tribal aesthetic traditions of India, in space and time. Very recently indeed has the forcefulness of the folk and tribal art caught the connoisseur's eye!

The oral cultural traditions that were rendered into script represent only a highly limited version of a much broader kaleidoscope of aesthetic traditions. But owing to their more obvious presence the written sources variously denoted as 'classical', 'canonical ', or 'shastric' became known as the mainstream of Indian culture – although these codified texts were no more than miniscule drops in the vast ocean of unrecorded oral cultural traditions and indigenous knowledge. These became the sole sources of understanding of Indian artistic traditions by the early European historians of India – and therefore the world. On the other hand the vast ocean of creative genius manifested for millennia by millions of people in the various religious, cultural and social contexts, not rendered into writing became known as 'minor', 'little', 'folk', 'tribal' and relegated into the background in a confusion of values. The cultural achievements of the anonymous artist and craftsman, far out in the villages, forests and secluded hills, were shadowed by a discriminative approach and ignored. And while this neglect and discrimination continued, another devil – of industrialization and mindless modernization and subsequently globalisation – spread its long tentacles wreaking havoc on and meticulously wiping out millennia old cultural traditions, thus sounding the death-knell of even the possibility of retrieving and recording these precious heritages.

This long neglect and wanton destruction of our folk and tribal heritage has been compounded by the unsavoury process of a pseudo-intellectual distinction between 'arts' and 'crafts' or 'fine arts' and 'decorative arts'. This led to a profound loss of repositories of rich ethnographic material bearing centuries old expression and symbolism. A macabre anti-aestheticism kept people from realizing that art can be present in one's work-day experience in terms of articles and objects of daily use. But in the folk-tribal milieu artistic activity is not a separate domain – it is inextricably linked to the mundane activities of everyday life to the production of utilitarian objects.

So collection of fast disappearing folk-tribal objets d'art remained more a question of conscience, sensibility and sensitivity rather than resources. And a collector of such art had to be a man with sensibility illumined by broad historical perspective, poetic perceptiveness and an intensity of feeling. And so was K.C. Aryan – an inspired if neglected collector and custodian of a veritable repertoire of folk and tribal art and artifacts – who realized the intrinsic worth and pricelessness of this indigenous heritage much before others. And the existence of Home of Folk Art – a museum of folk, tribal and neglected art that he set up in 1984 can surely be a source of solace, in this dismal scenario, to all sensitive, conscientious, right thinking people.

K. C. ARYAN AND HOME OF FOLK ART – THE MAN AND THE MUSEUM

A man of many parts – painter, sculptor, calligrapher, illustrator, art historian, art collector and founder of a museum – the essence of K.C. Aryan's amazing versatility lay in his deep feeling for India and it's unique art and cultural heritage. The raw vitality of his creativity and pioneering works springs from his auto-didactic knowledge of arts and crafts which was 'vast and encyclopaedic'. And for six decades this grand old man of Indian art tried to impress upon his fellow men, through his several books, exhibitions, paintings and a unique collection of folk and tribal objects, the inanity of neglecting and negating one's cultural traditions since these are the forces that shape a beautiful present. His mission was to instil artistic consciousness in the minds of the people and help them understand the aesthetic vision of the folk & tribal forms. His predilection for these forms came from the conviction of it's relevance not only because of it's immediate and spontaneous appeal but because he believed that this art formed the backbone of classical forms. To understand his mission and work one has to explore his roots.

Kishan Chand Aryan was born in Amritsar into a family of hereditary painters in 1919. His father, Lala Harnam Dass was a well known painter and a disciple of Bawa, the last painter to work in the Kangra style. Greatly influenced by his father, child Aryan spent hours sitting next to him dabbing colours on bits of paper. Another metier his father indulged in was metal to make copper plaques with religious themes. Thus he breathed art since infancy and learnt personal integrity from the life and mores of the simple, humble, sound-hearted craftsmen and artisans early in life. This also helped him withstand the tradition corroding forces of a wooden academic art and gave birth to an aesthetic vision and a creative urge that shaped his subsequent life. His father dissuaded him from following a profession that would leave him satiated but penniless but his love for art did not leave him any option. Entirely self-taught, without any formal training, he concentrated on acquiring mastery of skill and technique by practice and observation and the only resources he could fall back on were hard work, perseverence and determination. He found his vocation in illustrating and calligraphy which culminated in a study of the evolution of the *Devanagari* script as recorded in his book *Rekha* published in 1952, the only reference of its kind till date. The contemporary art scene that confronted young Aryan was in need of a desperate creative push to bridge the gap between a triumphant occidental sensibility and a traditional artistic heritage. And he brought into the light of intellectual comprehension the great life – disciplines behind the arts of another day and evolved an idiom that was contemporary yet linked to the realities of the Indian locale – an impressionist style using western techniques. His travels in 1958 in Europe and the Middle East provoked a thought process that resulted in experimentation in diverse media and pioneering work in collages, mesh-wire and metal assemblages. From a father who made metal plaques to a son creating metal assemblages, Aryan had come a full circle – and was awarded the *Lalit Kala Akademi Award* in 1964. In 1963, an associate of Le Corbusier upon seeing these works commented that "Indians will not be able to understand it for another 50 years!" And this trendsetting holds true for him in all spheres of work.

An experience of a classical dance performance by dancer Ram Gopal, as early as 1940, had ignited interest in the origin of art traditions and led to his art-historical explorations. This resulted in extensive travels into the remotest corners of the subcontinent, especially in the regions now known as Punjab, Himachal, Haryana and Rajasthan and he learned, imbibed and soaked in all that the folk and tribal milieu had to offer. During these travels he was exposed to the most appealing of arts and crafts which he initially sketched and later photographed, since he had no resources to buy them or space to keep them. This way he collected countless photographs of art and craft objects, mudwall paintings, temple murals, wood carvings, toys, pottery, jewellery etc. The murals of Punjab were entirely his discovery, which he preserved in book form before the actual specimens were whitewashed. And subsequently destroyed. Another remarkable contribution was drawing the connoisseur's attention to the 'bazaar school' of paintings from Punjab which can be seen today only in the London museums or in his collection. He soon realized that these millennia old folk and tribal traditions will not be able to withstand the onslaught of rapid industrialization that was penetrating the remotest habitations as the villagers were not conscious of the value of their traditional heritage. Even when they were, their conditions were too miserable – and Aryan witnessed many a charkha and woodcarvings being consumed in the fire, exquisite embroideries being converted to rags and vibrant folk bronzes being reshaped into door handles and fortunately managed to rescue a few. He knew that in another 50 years there would be no record of them. The awareness of their being lost into oblivion dawned upon him at that young age and he was gripped with a strong urge to salvage them for posterity. He was the first to recognize the relevance of these everyday arts at a time when collectors saw merit only in classical forms carrying the captions of Sunga, Maurya, Gupta, Pallava, Pala etc.. Thus motivated, and undaunted,

Aryan pooled all his resources to build up a unique collection of these objects of day-to-day use and this effort of a lifetime houses itself in his home-cum-museum; for future generations to see and draw inspiration from. Aryan had not only been collecting traditional artifacts but also writing about the unexplored areas of Indian art history. He collected these items when connoisseurs never deigned to look at them and wrote on them; when no scholar thought them worthy of any scholarship!

Aryan's scholarship highlighted the art of the unexplored areas and based on his personal collection and experiences in the field, he wrote *Folk Bronzes of North Western India* in 1973. In the foreword to this book Stella Kramrisch acknowledges Aryan's contribution to this field, stating that, "K.C.Aryan is singularly equipped in writing on them, having lived, seen and collected many of the images on the spot and being a practising artist." He painstakingly amassed the largest collection of 'Hanuman' images in the country and this forms the basis of his most celebrated work – *Hanuman in Art and Mythology* – published in 1975. His book on the 'Cultural Heritage of Punjab' from a historical perspective remains a pioneering work. These unequivocally established Aryan as a scholar and collector of rare and mostly extinct folk, tribal and neglected objets d'art. However his collecting career had started much earlier in the junk shops of Lahore, when teenaged Aryan went without his meals for a day to spend his last eight rupees on an embroidered Chinese silk ensemble, now worth a fortune!

And notwithstanding his remarkable contribution in the field of Indian painting and sculpture it is as an art collector that he has made an unusual and unparalleled contribution to the Indian cultural heritage – although it is essentially just an outgrowth of his innately aesthetic temperament. Home of Folk Art – that he set up in his small artistically designed red brick house in a quiet corner of the sprawling urban estate of Gurgaon has the distinction of being the first institution of its kind in the country. A unique thing about this enterprise is that the arts and crafts of Punjab, Himachal and Haryana have been exhibited for the first time in the form of a gallery. Another factor contributing to the uniqueness is that of it being the only museum of art in Haryana. So the seminal interest developed in a penniless young boy wandering in the streets of the *Kabari bazars* in Lahore reached its fullest measure in the founding of this rare institution. In his unflinching zeal for art collection lies a worthwhile lesson for art historians, collectors, critics and practitioners, the message being: contemplation of art and its appreciation is a question of conscience and not commercial expediency.

A visionary *per se*, K.C. Aryan may well be remembered as a man who rolled up ten lives work into one! The artist in Aryan has eternally captured the spiritual attitude of the aesthetic milieu of the Indian people by pouring their collective consciousness into pursuits and a lifestyle that are as inspiring as they are difficult to excel. K.C. Aryan never drew away from his roots. All through his long artistic 'career', there is the underlying current and continual influence of rediscovery and reinterpretation of traditional strains in Indian art and culture. His contribution to Indian art and culture is comparable to Tagore's but unfortunately his milieu did not help him being recognised as deservingly as Tagore's did.

THE COLLECTION AND ITS SIGNIFICANCE

Comprising of objects, beautiful and intriguing, painstakingly collected from across the length and breadth of the country, or rather the subcontinent, the museum modestly attempts to reflect the entire gamut of the Indian folk and tribal ethos in all its nuances. The collection amazes one by its sheer size and bewildering range. The collection simply overflows, literally and metaphorically, being unable to be contained by the space assigned to it, physically as well as symbolically. Every inch of wall space, every corner of the room is crammed with something precious, old, rare and of exquisite craftsmanship. Still largely confined to storage and minimally displayed, rather informally and without much method, the gross lack of space and facilities the collection suffers from is made up only by the soulful care and almost ritualistic devotion of the people who look after it.

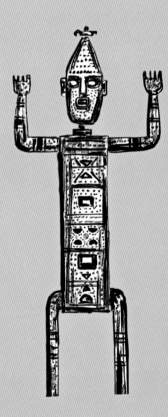

The collection hardly leaves any crevice of the folk and tribal paraphernalia unexplored and the items, mostly extinct, range from the esoteric to the mundane, the sacred to the profane, the crude to the refined and the ritualistic to the utilitarian. And each bears the undeniable mark of a connoisseur and reflects the subtle responses of a sensitive, aesthetic soul captured and swayed as it was by the exuberance of our folk and tribal imagination – striking a deep chord in the most naive of viewers. Each piece seems to have been hand picked by a person who cared for the craftsman and his craftsmanship and this is what sets the collection apart from all the other larger and better displayed ones in the country. And on display are thousands of fascinating objects that, chronologic ambiguities notwithstanding, belong to a period between fourth century B.C. to early twentieth century.

The museum is a rich repertoire of the rarest folk bronzes, especially from Himachal, spectacular tribal wood carvings, functional iron artifacts from various socio-cultural locales, antique terracotta figurines and toys, myriad schools of folk & bazaar paintings, rare book covers and fabulous folk embroideries. Exquisite Punjab *Phulkari*s, Pahari *Rumal*s from Himachal, Bengal *Kanthas*, Swat shawls together with a plethora of folk textiles from other regions vie for space with each other. The different categories of rare folk paintings and manuscripts, though grotesque in concept and strong in colour and at complete variance with the sophistication of miniatures, hold a unique pride of place in the K.C. Aryan collection with their vitality and distinct artistic individuality. Eclectic in nature, the collection also includes various ritualistic and religious art objects like *tantrik* drawings and *yantra*s, the rare *Pataka*s depicting *Devi*s and *Yogini*s (the only ones of their kind preserved in any museum), numerous tools and implements and umpteen minor arts. Lithographs from Amritsar dating from the early British period are amongst the museum's prized possessions – the only other pieces being in the Archer Collection at Victoria and Albert Museum, London. Cutting across several media, from the invincible bronze to the fragile paper, is a special thematic collection of 'Hanuman' images from all over India, Nepal and even South-East Asia – the single largest in the world. This celebrated collection comprises paintings, bronzes, silver pendants, armlets, *pataka*s, embroideries, woodcarvings, stone images, dramatic masks, etc. of the simian God. A massive collection of life-size Shiva heads or *Mukhalingam*s from Karnataka, originally used as phallic covers, compete with an equally imposing collection of countless Durga *Mahisasuramardini*s. Amongst the other highlights are the *Ganjifa* – the traditional playing cards, and the exquisitely worked card puppets – the only ones of its type – from 17th century Jaisalmer.

Now, what is the significance of a collection such as this? How does one place it into a proper perspective?

India, with its myriad strands of millennia old, now endangered, living cultural traditions has developed an extremely complex socio-cultural and religious fabric over time. Almost equally traditional has been an apathy towards the so called 'folk', 'tribal' or 'minor' cultures since antiquity. However these artistic expressions, unconfined as they are by canonical rules, emanate a tremendous vitality, spontaneity and freedom of expression – reflecting the collective consciousness of the people they are born out of. Being far more intensive and extensive in character than most other folk/tribal collections in India this collection strongly embodies this 'collective consciousness' of our people and the rich folk/tribal moorings of our culture. With its rich ethnographic content the collection has an overarching anthropological significance that can hardly be overemphasized.

This apart the collection is a most deserving tribute to the unnumbered anonymous artists and artisans of our soil through the centuries. In it are manifest the creative genius and artistic expression of countless unknown potters, weavers, embroiderers, painters, sculptors and other craftspersons of this country 'whose names and identities have been lost in the mists of time' and whose artistry is comparable to, if not excelling, the best of its kind found anywhere in the history of human civilization.

Also in a society like India having ancient time-culture relationships, the folk, tribal and urban have existed side by side as a continuum influencing each other and giving birth to composite systems of art, religion and folklore. With a plethora of transitional forms, belonging unequivocally to neither folk, tribal or classical, that pose a challenge to classification to the most erudite the collection holds an invaluable key to the delineation of numerous ethnological/art historical evolutions, transitions and ramifications.

Finally under encroaching global influences India is fast losing its traditional way of life and all the beauty and creativity that accompanied it. Customised hand made indigenous artifacts – whether folk, tribal or classical – are being lost for good under the onslaught of initially industrialization and presently consumerism and homogenization sadly reminding one of the dictum of Ruskin that "industry without art is brutality". Also having their fair share in this dismal drama are indiscriminate vandalism and mindless 'development' programmes, often state sponsored. And so such carefully salvaged museumised remnants of material culture as these remain the only recourse to the past for posterity.

Thus this collection fills up some very important pages in the human history of the Indian subcontinent. The hundreds of small things that make up its ethnological matrix record the every day life of past centuries and communities and tell us interesting stories from the past. And can help us to understand ourselves and our origins better. Its potential can be harnessed to educate the newer alienated generations and inspire posterity regarding our bio-cultural diversity. It not only preserves valuable art and cultural traditions but also extends an art form which, by virtue of its raw vitality, makes serious inroads into our modern sensibility. More importantly it holds within itself and enriches us with the indigenous knowledge systems so crucial to evolving more organic and sustainable development processes, culturally and ecologically sound, for the present and the future.

WHAT NEXT? THE ROAD AHEAD

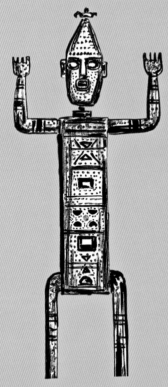

K. C. Aryan took the pioneering task of salvaging this wonderful heritage. An equally pioneering task of preservation and promotion of this heritage and making the world aware of it remains. The hurdles towards this goal are plentiful in number and varied in nature.

Neither was K. C. Aryan a *maharaja* nor is his Home of Folk Art a Government museum with unlimited funds. The constraints and the lack of resources are too stark to overlook. There is hardly any space, let alone the essential facilities like showcases and airconditioning, for display or storage that befits such a precious collection and too limited funds to redeem the situation. Security aspects add to the apprehensions. And as the years pass by in mobilising public opinion and enlightening the authorities the priceless artifacts lie either strewn in the open or locked in trunks, slowly consumed by worms. One can imagine a buyer from a foreign museum going berserk over the items but Aryan, or his family, never thought of selling this hard-earned collection or acknowledging it in monetary terms. Their only dream and desire is to see it housed in a proper museum in India and they continue to live with the hope that, by some freak of destiny, it would be realized. But this dire need to preserve that motivates the resourceless family, against all odds, escapes the enlightened administration and modern culture *pandit*s who have till date done precious little to even acknowledge or encourage this effort.

Ironically enough, Indians have traditionally been apathetic to their art heritage. Most of it has been preserved for us and brought to our somewhat indifferent notice by art historians, scholars and critics from the West. Sadly enough the position in independent India has not changed significantly, though a fashion has lately struck roots in the elite sensibility to masquerade as self-styled custodians and promoters of traditional art by squandering money on ill-conceived plans, policies and programmes. The neo-elitist culture seeks to keep alive our great heritage by awesome art 'circuses' while authorities turn a blind eye to systematic vandalism towards the rarest relics of art. And funds as well as conscientious, courageous, illumined people who could be instrumental in saving a heritage, as unique as K. C. Aryan's collection, remain elusive and the contribution of Aryan goes unnoticed. Vain artistic pursuits and glossy coffee tablers prevail while true artistic endeavour and genuine scholarship continue to remain marginalized, until a quiet death in penury in the crowd of pseudo-intellectualism. Comprehensive aesthetic sensibilities are becoming scarce and the cultural horizon is growingly subject to a myopic elitist coterie that creates a hypocritical artistic ambience without relating to the organic cultural ethos of the Indian milieu. Standing at the forefront such czars of culture hardly have the sensibility to appreciate either the 'intuitive mind' or the 'inner eye' that makes the true Indian aesthetic culture. But hope lives on. And on...

Maybe one day, hopefully not too late, the significance of salvaging this national heritage for a second time will draw the attention of decision makers. And public opinion mobilized and enough sense of pride awakened in Indian polity to motivate them to undertake cultural conservation projects throughout the country as a national commitment to posterity. And Home of Folk Art should be housed in a new space commensurate with its character, size and significance. With proper infrastructure and facilities and planned, systematic preservational and promotional activities it should be reborn a glorious museum of mankind to play its rightful role for the future generations. It is a heritage the whole nation as well as the world should be proud of and the onus of placing it on the pedestal it deserves to be on, lies not with the family alone or with the state but with each and every individual or organization in the world – that would be fortunate enough to know of its existence.

In the stark dismal scenario, after years of neglect and indifference, an opportunity such as this to publish the 'Masterpieces From The K.C. Aryan Collection' is indeed a reason for immense rejoicing. An unprecedented exposure of a global dimension, the publication will create awareness about this unique Indian heritage all over the world and help connoisseurs, collectors, critics, scholars and art-lovers see and appreciate, for the first time, some of the rare and unknown masterpieces of folk and tribal art that form part of this collection – and perhaps reassess the aesthetic richness of Indian folk and tribal traditions.

It is a huge recognition, however late, of the priceless contribution of K.C. Aryan towards conservation of Indian cultural heritage. It will help to carry to distant places and perhaps more deserving ears the story of this collection and its present plight and its message of concern for conservation of cultural relics and traditions. And we hope that all intelligent, sensible, sensitive art-loving people from across the world will come forward and prevent this rare remnant of art heritage from passing into oblivion.

B.N. Aryan
Director

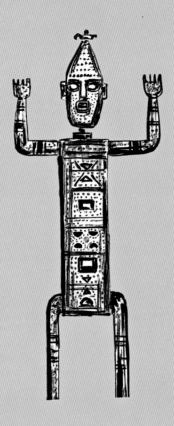

NEVER DOUBT THAT A SMALL GROUP OF
THOUGHTFUL COMMITTED CITIZENS
CAN CHANGE THE WORLD:
INDEED, IT IS THE ONLY THING THAT EVER DOES.

Margaret Mead

Protective Jain yantra,
Rajasthan, 16th century.
Coiled bodies of twin serpents
joined together enclose a yantra
inscribed with mystical mantras,
invoked for protection.

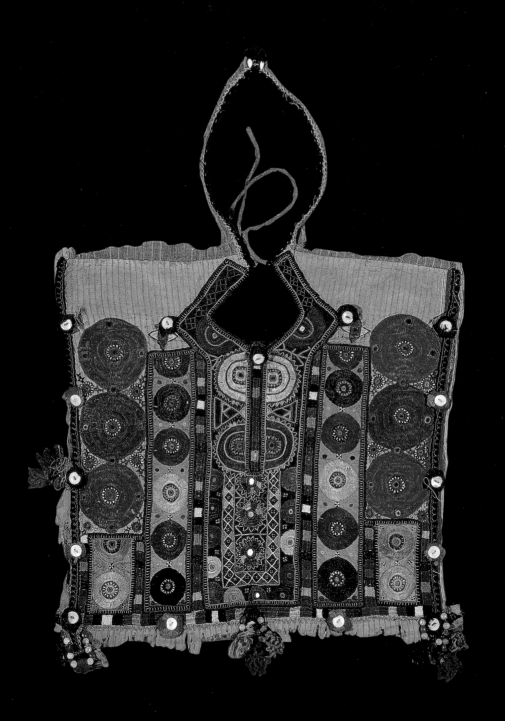